WALKING THE
EAST MOJAVE DESERT

The real desert . . . is a land whose character is hidden except to those who come with friendliness and understanding.
To those who come to the desert with friendliness, it gives friendship. To those who come with courage, it gives new strength of character. Those seeking relaxation find release from the world of man-made troubles. For those seeking beauty, the desert offers nature's rarest artistry. This is the desert that men and women learn to love.

Randall Henderson
Desert Magazine

Walking the
East Mojave Desert

A Visitor's Guide to
Mojave National Park

John McKinney and Cheri Rae

HarperCollins *West*

A division of HarperCollins *Publishers*

HarperCollins*West* and the author, in association with the Rainforest Action Network, will facilitate the planting of two trees for every one tree used in the manufacture of this book.

WALKING THE EAST MOJAVE: A VISITOR'S GUIDE TO MOJAVE NATIONAL PARK. Copyright ©1994 by John McKinney. All rights reserved. Printed in the United States of America. No part of this book may be used or reproduced in any manner whatsoever without written permission except in the case of brief quotations embodied in critical articles and reviews. For information address HarperCollins*Publishers,* 10 East 53rd Street, New York, New York 10022.

This book was previously published as *East Mojave Desert* by Olympus Press in 1989.

FIRST HARPERCOLLINS EDITION

LIBRARY OF CONGRESS CATALOGING-IN-PUBLICATION DATA
McKinney, John
     Walking the east Mojave: a visitor's guide to Mojave
    National Park / John McKinney and Cheri Rae. — 1st
    HarperCollins ed.
      p. cm. — (Walking the West)
    Originally published: East Mojave desert: a visitor's
    guide. Olympus Press, 1989.
      ISBN 0-06-258512-6 (pbk.: alk. paper)
     1. East Mojave National Scenic Area (Calif.)—
    Guidebooks. 2. Natural history—California—East
    Mojave National Scenic Area—guidebooks. 3. Desert
    ecology—California—East Mojave National Scenic
    Area—Guidebooks. I. Title. II. Series.
    F868.M65M37 1994   93-26564
    917.94'950453—dc20   CIP

94 95 96 97 **CWI**   10 9 8 7 6 5 4 3 2 1

This edition is printed on acid-free paper that meets the American National Standards Institute Z39.48 Standard.

ACKNOWLEDGMENTS

For providing an introduction to the East Mojave, its places and politics, we'd like to thank the chairs of the California Desert Protection League: Judy Anderson, Elden Hughes, and Jim Dodson. For hiking with us in searing heat and unexpected snowstorms, and for valuable information about the area, a big thank you to John Bailey, Jim Foote, Harold Johnson, Arthur Smith, and Renee Straub of the U.S. Bureau of Land Management. For research assistance, a tip of the hat to Dr. Gerald Scherba and the Desert Studies Center. For Old West hospitality, our sincere thanks to Jerry Freeman and Roxanne Lang.

CREDITS

Design and typography by Jim Cook
Cartography by Susan Kuromiya

PHOTO CREDITS

Automobile Club of Southern California, 16, 46, 64, 70; California Department of Parks and Recreation: 124, 167; California Desert Studies Center, 182; California State Library, 82, 85; Mojave River Valley Museum: J. Amari collection, 18; C. Gilliam collection, 42; Bruce collection, 34, 99; Billingham collection, 63, Ives, U.S. Government, 100; Cochran collection, 106; Burnau/Pendergast collection, 113; Pinnell collection, 127; Mary Beal collection, 130; Brenck collection, 159; MacFarlane collection, 160, MacFarlane/Prather collection, 175; Mojave River Valley Museum collection, 194; San Bernardino County Library, Needles, 36, 37, 102, 104, 111, 158, 198; Steele Photographic Service, 18, 20, 102, 108, 110, 133, 149, 161; *Trailer Life* magazine, 30; U.S. Borax Corporation: 89; U.S. Bureau of Land Management, 12, 13, 21, 33, 34, 49, 50, 74, 76, 78, 83, 85, 86, 87, 88 , 89, 90, 91, 93, 95, 96, 104, 112, 114, 120, 132, 138, 139, 154, 156, 166, 168, 169, 181, 183, 186. Other photos are by the authors.

Table of Contents

Walking the East Mojave Desert

THE VERY NOTION of walking the desert in general, and the East Mojave in particular, is a surprising one to some people—even to some avid hikers. The desert that seems so huge from a car, can seem intimidating on foot.

Apparently not that intimidating though; reader response to John McKinney's *Los Angeles Times* hiking columns about the East Mojave proved to be enthusiastic to say the least! More walks "way out there" readers demanded.

With such a desert, the visitor really needs two views: the broad view offered by an auto tour, the intimate view offered by a sojourn afoot.

Throughout this guide, we've suggested some favorite walks: to Amboy Crater off old Route 66; along willow-lined Aiken Wash; to—and into—the unusual Lava Tube; around the grounds of the old Zzyzx resort; along the Mojave River near Camp Cady and many more.

These walks are leg-stretchers, informal wanderings, part of the grand tour of the East Mojave. We hope that you heed some of our suggestions, get out of car and walk as much as possible.

This desert also offers some longer, half-day and all-day walks. Some of these walks are suitable for the whole family, others are for experienced hikers in good condition.

(For the very experienced desert hiker, there are some excellent Class 2 and Class 3 climbs and cross-country routes. Providence and New York peaks are two fine climbs; however, these and other peak-bagging expeditions require skills and route-finding abilities beyond that of most visitors, and we decided they were beyond the scope of this guide. By all means, if you are one of these experienced hikers, get yourself some topo maps and an ample water supply and go for it!)

For the average day hiker, there's a week or two's worth of wonderful walking in the East Mojave. From the cool, mysterious environs of Mitchell Caverns to the magnificent Joshua Tree forest and the boulder-strewn Caruthers Canyon, the East Mojave Desert offers the hiker a surprising diversity of terrain.

This desert has a way of making every trip an adventure. If you like the idea of walking to places where it seems there's no one else for miles around, or where you could swear no one has ever been before, the East Mojave may be just the place for you.

PART I

Welcome
To The
East Mojave

It is in the fascination of the unknowable , in the challenge of some old unbroken secret that the charm of the desert consists.

—Joseph Smeaton Chase

If this land could speak . . .

what stories it would tell!

IF THIS LAND COULD SPEAK, what stories it would tell! Tales of Indians and Spanish explorers, trappers and trailblazers, pioneers and gold miners and cattle ranchers and restless spirits. It would speak of the past, when men lived harmoniously with this place; working hard with their hands, traversing it quietly, carefully, with a little fear and a lot of respect, and leaving behind little more than tracks in the sand. It would tell of booms and busts, lone prospectors and great armies, those who scratched at the land and scarred it, those who lived with the land and loved it.

If this land could speak, it would remind us, we last minute arrivals on the scene, that it has witnessed profound changes in form and substance, change by firestorm and flood and the passage of millions of years. It would speak of the great oceans and tropical forests that once covered it and speak of the cactus and creosote, jimson and juniper and the thousand and one living things that bloom and blossom and cover it today. It would speak of the great numbers of animals that have inhabited this place—some now extinct, others whose very existence is endangered.

And yet this land that cannot speak calls to us. Some of us have been drawn to its silent places, some of us have let the desert fill our hearts. It's a call of the wild that can't be heard, only felt and experienced.

A land of towering peaks and shimmering sands, the ancient land of the East Mojave.

And so it's we humans who speak, sometimes eloquently, sometimes with great disregard for the beauty of the English language, for this land. Today, the silent places are the subject of noisy debate among miners, ranchers, environmentalists, fundamentalists, land planners, politicians, actors and actresses, offroad vehicle riders, rockhounds, birdwatchers, hikers, mountain bikers, motorcyclists, herpetologists, photographers, astronomers . . . in short, just about everyone who has ever set foot in

11

the desert has an opinion about this land, how it should be managed and who should manage it.

"If you would experience a landscape, you must go alone into it and sit down somewhere quietly and wait for it to come in its own good time to you," writes Paul Gruchow in *The Necessity of Empty Places*. We propose that you visit some of the silent places of the East Mojave—and take your own sweet time of it.

And when the land speaks to you and you are moved—and you will be moved because no one who visits the wonders of this desert land is left unmoved—you, too, will want to speak for the land. And when you speak we hope it is with a clear voice, a strong voice, a voice that speaks from the heart of the beauty you have seen and of the necessity for preserving this beauty in a world that has already lost far too many wild, beautiful silent places.

—J.M. & C.R.

Introduction

THE EAST MOJAVE is a desert of unusual diversity, a land of great mesas and mountain ranges, sand dunes and extinct volcanoes. It's a land that's easy to like, hard to know.

The intent of this guide is to help you explore this vast unknown land. In the past, information about this desert has been as scarce as water in these parts. While the area has in recent years often made the news over such controversies as mining activity, off-highway vehicle use, and whether the desert should be "upgraded" to national park status, these headlines have offered few clues to its beauty and recreational possibilities.

Besides introducing the reader to the scenery, an attempt has been made to mine the rich legends and lore of the East Mojave. This land was once populated far more extensively than it is now (quite the reverse of most of the rest of California!) and the colorful characters who lived and worked here are a book in themselves.

In 1980, the East Mojave achieved some national prominence when Congress set aside 1.5 million acres in the California desert and designated it the East Mojave National Scenic Area. It was the first of the nation's Scenic Areas (among other areas later set aside were Mono Lake, the Santa Rosa Mountains and the Columbia River Gorge). The East Mojave was assigned to the U.S. Bureau of Land Management, an agency under the Department of the Interior.

While "National Scenic Area" status put the East Mojave on the map as something special, the designation lacked the allure to most Americans of those two magic words: "National Park." Visitation remained light (though annually increasing) during the 1980s and early 1990s.

Two groups that did not ignore—and, in fact, obsessed about—the East Mojave were planners and politicians. Planners, both governmental and environmental advocates, compiled massive documents about what all of us—miners, motorists, mountain climbers and more—would/could/should do in the desert. Planners, in the peculiar jargon of their trade, spoke of UPAS (Unusual Plant Assemblages), WSAs (Wilderness Study Areas) and FLPMA (Federal Land Policy and Management Act), as in "How will we manage the UPAS in the WSAs under FLMPA?"

Politicians—particularly California's U.S. senators—continually beat the drum for more—or less—federal protection for the desert. Lobbyists for ranching and mining interests, the Sierra Club and the National Rifle Association, and many more special interest groups, tried to convince legislators of their particular views of the East Mojave. Somewhere between the planners and the politicos is the public. Planners and politicians have their own documents; this guide is for the rest of us, for you, the public.

How many of us actually visit the East Mojave Desert? No one has a truly accurate count or even a particularly good guess. Unlike some popular western national parks where visitors pass through toll gates, and bureaucrats measure use in millions of "visitor days," no one in this vast desert collects admission fees. The eastern Mojave has many entrances—making a visitor count difficult, if not impossible. One thing for certain: the East Mojave is not called "The Lonesome Triangle" for nothing.

Surveys report that as many as one in three Southern Californians venture into the desert each year, but only a fraction of these adventurers head for the East Mojave. Some 17 million people live less than a four-hour's drive from the East Mojave but few city dwellers can locate this desert land on the map, and even fewer visit.

While the vastness of this land can intimidate, by exploring the East Mojave a little at a time, you'll soon come to know and love this special place. It's a half-day's drive from the metropolis, a world apart.

Access

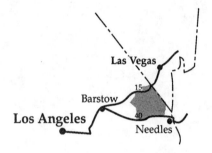

THE EAST MOJAVE DESERT is bounded north and south by two major Interstates, I-15 and I-40, and on the east by U.S. Highway 95. Just south of I-40 is one of the longest remaining stretches of old Route 66. The area bounded by these three highways has been dubbed "The Lonesome Triangle."

Motorists who speed along these super-highways in air-conditioned comfort rarely think of the sturdy pioneers who made their way across this barren territory a century ago. These pioneers knew there were no supply outlets where they could expect to re-supply along the way, so they carried sufficient food and water.

Desert towns have since mushroomed, and services have been established in many places throughout the Mojave; still, some modern-day travelers express reluctance to venture into the desert. While it's true that services are widely spaced in the desert, undue concern about becoming stranded far from civilization is unwarranted.

Access roads to the East Mojave pass through many small towns, where essentials—food, gas, water, telephones—are available. Good planning and advance preparation, and perhaps some on-the-spot resourcefulness will enrich your Mojave adventure.

Desert drivers often complain that the long, straight and virtually unchanging highway is monotonous and boring to drive. Your travel through the desert is more pleasant, however, when you take a little time to explore the sights located right off the highway. Near the East Mojave, visit a beautiful canyon, an archeological excavation site, a fossil-laden ancient lakebed—even old-time diners and abandoned gas stations along historic old Route 66.

Remember, it's all a matter of perspective: one person's interminable stretch of highway is another's road to adventure. The journey can be as important—and as enjoyable—as the destination.

The Automobile Club of Southern California was instrumental in mapping, signing and improving desert roads.

CHAPTER ONE

Interstate 15

I-15 IS THE NORTHERN BOUNDARY of the East Mojave Desert. The primarily 65-mph speed limit highway is the major route taken between Barstow and the state line by Las Vegas-bound travelers from Southern California. It's also a stretch of highway that provides access to a number of unexpectedly pleasant desert destinations.

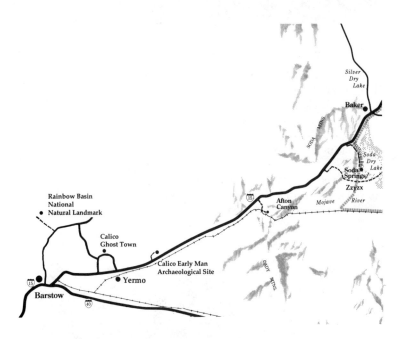

Near Barstow

Barstow Depot, circa 1880; situated at the junction of the California Southern and the Atlantic and Pacific Railways

I-15 anchors the westernmost point of the East Mojave at Barstow, population 20,000, where fast-food stands, restaurants and motels line Main Street. It's a major supply point, a place to purchase food, gas, film and provisions before you head into the desert for an extended stay.

Barstow Station on the east side of town is the locale of a gargantuan McDonald's serving up Big Macs in converted railroad cars. The station also has a tourist information outpost.

During the 1950s, America launched its Interstate Highway System. These gals and CHP officers are celebrating the opening of I-15.

Desert Information

The California Desert Information Center is a logical first stop on a west-east desert tour.

The first stop. East Mojave travelers find maps, books, touring information and natural history displays.

Maps, informative brochures, information about area camping, lodging and desert attractions, along with a selection of guidebooks are available. Nature exhibits and a personable staff help the visitor get oriented.

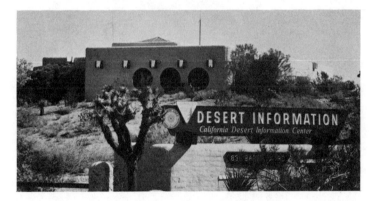

California Desert Information Center
831 Barstow Road (take the Central
Barstow exit off I-15, one block north)
(619) 256-8617
Hours: 9-5 Monday through Friday;
9-4 weekends

Mojave River Valley Museum

Founded by local citizens in 1964, this eclectic museum is dedicated to preserving and interpreting the heritage of the Mojave River Valley. Exhibits include archeological artifacts from the nearby Calico Early Man Site; locally found gemstones and minerals, including agates, jaspers and turquoise; and photographs of city pioneers. A collection of publications and local crafts are available for purchase at the museum.

1912 view of the Barstow Garage, which sold Red Crown — "the Gasoline of Quality."

Mojave River Valley Museum,
Corner of Barstow Road and Virgina Way,
Barstow (two blocks southwest of the
California Desert Information Center)
(619) 256-5452
Hours: 11-4 daily;
closed Tuesday and Wednesday

Rainbow Basin

The designation as a National Natural Landmark is a tip-off, but nothing can prepare you for the sight of the spectacular geologic formations, or the exquisite colorations of Rainbow Basin.

Some 15 million years ago, grasslands filled Rainbow Basin, which was populated by saber-toothed tigers, mastodons, camels, three-toed horses and even rhinoceros.

Folded and faulted landscape of Rainbow Basin invites exploration. Closer examination reveals the fossil remains of many animals embedded in the rocks.

Their fossil remains are encased in the sedimentary rock that once formed the lakebed. As a result of intense geologic activity over the millenia, what was once at the bottom of the lake is now a series of folded, faulted, colorful hills. The subtle colorations, the greens and browns, are due to the differing oxidation rates of iron.

These towering hills, exquisitely formed and appearing to be hand-painted, are seen from the signed 3-mile, one-way loop drive.

Rainbow Basin National
Natural Landmark,
10 miles north of Barstow. (From Highway
58 in Barstow, take Fort Irwin Road north
5.5 miles to Fossil Bed Road. Follow signs
approximately 3 miles to the Landmark;
take 3-mile-long scenic drive.)

Calico Ghost Town

Calico, a one-time boomtown that produced more than $86 million from its silver mines, went bust just after the turn of the century. The town has been restored, and today it's a regional park operated by San Bernardino County.

The town features several Western-style shops, restaurants and attractions, including a mine tour, playhouse, railroad and museum. Some of the original 19th-Century buildings are still standing: the saloon, town office, country store and general store.

Calico hosts a number of regularly scheduled events, including a Hullabaloo (the weekend before Easter), the Spring Music Festival (Mother's Day weekend) and Calico Days (Columbus Day weekend).

This Wild West tourist stop attracts vistors from all over the world. On any given day, you may overhear French, German, Japanese or Italian.

The 1880 mining district of Calico produced $86 million worth of silver and supported a population of more than 4,000 before the boom faded.

Calico Ghost Town,
7.5 miles east of Barstow
(Exit I-15 at the Ghost Town Road exit; follow signs 3 miles north to the park.)
Fees for parking and admission.

P.O. Box 638
Yermo, CA 92398
(619) 254-2122
Hours: 9-5 daily

Calico Early Man Site

The stone tools of Pinto man, estimated to have lived on the shores of Lake Manix, circa 20,000 B.C. Although no human bones have ever been found at this site, these tools offer evidence of early man's habitation.

Prehistoric stone tools found at the Calico Early Man Archeological Site—scrapers, hand picks, choppers and the like—have been estimated by some to be up to 200,000 years old. The site's authenticity is highly controversial among anthropologists and archeologists, who heatedly debate the topic of Early Arrivals vs. Late Arrivals.

Nevertheless, Calico was the only place in North America where the famed archeologist/ paleontologist, Dr. Louis S. B. Leakey, chose to work. Known primarily for his work in Olduvai Gorge in East Africa, Leakey directed the excavation of the site from 1963 until his death in 1972. The National Geographic Society funded the project.

A visit to this site is an introduction to the tedious, methodical work of archeologists, a process unknown to many of us. Working with hand tools no bigger than toothbrushes and awls, archeologists

---

Calico Early Man Archeological Site
15 miles northeast of Barstow via I-15
(From the Minneola Road exit, follow
the signs north 2 1/2 miles along graded
dirt roads to the site)
Hours: open for guided tours Wednesday
1:30 and 3:30pm; Thursday-Sunday 9:30
and 11:30am and 1:30 and 3:30pm;
closed Monday and Tuesday
For group tours: write
Friends of Calico Early Man Site,
P.O. Box 535, Yermo, CA 92398.

The hand-held tools of the archeologist, who conducts painstaking work with the utmost care. The Early Man Site is one of the few places in America where visitors can view archeological work.

have recovered some 11,400 artifacts, moved uncounted tons of earth, kept meticulous records, and dug some 26 feet into the earth—three inches at a time.

A tour of the site is guaranteed to raise incomprehensible questions about the origins of human life and the passage of an unfathomably long period of time. It's an experience that is simultaneously enlightening and disturbing, inspiring and quite profound.

Tour leader Jeff Stark explains how Dr. Louis S.B. Leakey ordered archeological work to be conducted, one square foot at a time. This digging site is 25 feet deep.

Afton Canyon

The way the light plays on rugged walls of Afton Canyon prompted one ranger to comment, "Every time I come through here it looks different."

Afton Canyon is an integral component of the East Mojave ecosystem. Afton Canyon can be a pleasant place for a day hike or an extended stay (for greater detail, see Chapter 19 on the Mojave River Basin).

The canyon features a steep-walled gorge cut by the once-mighty Mojave River, and is often referred to as "the Grand Canyon of the Mojave." The river runs here year-round, allowing cottonwoods and other riparian vegetation to flourish.

Afton Canyon,
33 miles east of Baker (Take the Afton turnoff from I-15, then the 3-mile dirt and gravel road that's washboard in places; parking in Afton Campground)

Soda Springs / Zzyzx

Formerly a cavalry outpost and later a health resort run by radio minister Doc Springer, Soda Springs today is occupied by the California Desert Studies Center, a field station of the California State University, which was established in 1976 in cooperation with the Bureau of Land Management. The self-contained, energy-efficient facilities include classrooms, science labs, a complete kitchen and dormitory space.

Originally conceived as a research facility for use by university faculty and students, the center has evolved into an educational retreat for those interested in all facets of desert study.

Reservations are essential. The public can sign up for classes through the Office of Extended Education, California State University San Bernardino, CA 92407; (714) 887-7667.

Desert-oriented school and community groups can make reservations for accomodations through the Biology Department, California State University Fullerton, Fullerton, CA 92634; (714) 773-2428.

This colorful sign once pointed the way to Doc Springer's place. Today, I-15 travelers are intrigued by the less provocative Caltrans Zzyzx sign.

Regularly scheduled two-hour weekend tours of the Soda Springs facilities are offered. Tours include information about the area's natural history, human habitation, plants and animals, as well as insights into the former resort's history.

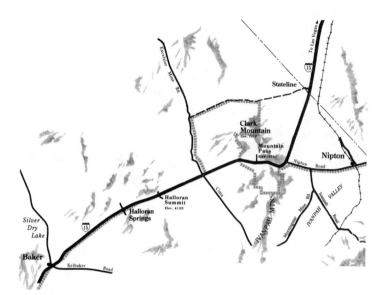

Soda Springs/Zzyzx/California
Desert Studies Center,
60 miles northeast of Barstow
(Exit I-15 at Zzyzx Road, south on
unpaved, graded road for 4 miles
to the center)

Baker

A small desert town, Baker is a good point to fill up your gas tank, purchase supplies, and make last-minute preparations before entering the East Mojave Desert. Accommodations and food are available in Baker; for a tasty surprise, stop at the Mad Greek restaurant. Order a Greek salad, a souvlaki or zucchini sticks and marvel at your good fortune; imagine finding such tasty food and pleasant surroundings in what many would consider the middle of nowhere. Across the street looms the world's tallest thermometer: 134 feet high, not coincidentally reaching 134°, the highest reported temperature in the northern hemisphere recorded nearby in Death Valley.

An unexpected oasis, offering air-conditioned comfort, good food and pleasant atmosphere— at the east end of Baker.

Baker is a good departure point for desert exploration. Highway 127 heads north to Death Valley. To begin your East Mojave adventure, however, take Kelbaker Road, which heads southeast of I-15 out of Baker and takes you straight to Kelso Depot (34.5 miles), and Kelso Dunes (44.7 miles) in the Scenic Area. (See Chapter 12.)

Halloran Springs and Halloran Summit, two extremely small settlements just off I-15, between Baker and Cima Road, do offer gas stations and water, but little else in terms of provisions or supplies.

At the Cima Road exit is a small settlement known as Valley Wells; facilities include food, water, gas, a small store and a phone. Sunshine Store, formerly a Stuckey's, is a good rendezvous point in this part of the East Mojave.

Baker
60 miles northeast of Barstow
(Exit I-15 at Baker Boulevard)

Nipton is the kind of desert town that often appears on television or newspapers as a human interest spot. The town's motto is "Where the past is present." It's perfectly appropriate, especially when the midnight freight train rumbles through.

Purchase provisions and maps at the Trading Post. Hotel Nipton, where silent film star Clara Bow was a frequent guest, is a pleasant Southwestern-style bed-and-breakfast. For a hedonistic desert treat, the hotel even offers an outdoor hot tub.

Moon over Nipton. A place for rest, relaxation and reflecting on the beauty of the desert.

Nipton
(exit I-15 at Nipton Road;
10 miles to the town)
Contact Nipton Station, Route #1,
P.O. Box 357, Nipton, CA 92364;
(619) 856-2335

Stateline

Beyond the turnoff to Nipton, I-15 bends north and heads for Vegas. But long before Glitter City, the highway takes you to aptly named Stateline on the California-Nevada border. Here you'll find—"can't miss" would perhaps be a better way to put it—Whiskey Pete's, a casino-hotel-restaurant-truckstop in ersatz Wild West decor, and boasting of "Nevada's loosest slots." Pete's sister, The Prima Donna Casino and Hotel, also vies for your attention.

Campgrounds off Interstate 15

Barstow/Calico KOA Campground
7 miles northeast of Barstow via I-15 and
Ghost Town Road
(619) 254-2311
72 tent and RV spaces

Calico Ghost Town Regional Park
1 1/2 miles southwest of Calico off I-15
(619) 254-2122
200 tent and RV spaces

Afton Canyon
35 miles northeast of Barstow off I-15 on
Dunn Road
(619) 256-3591
22 tent and RV spaces

Owl Canyon
10 miles north of Barstow via Highway 58
and Irwin Road (just south of
Rainbow Basin)
(619) 256-3591
31 tent and RV spaces

*Camping in the
East Mojave is
limited to
previously
disturbed sites.*

Caltrans Rest Areas on Interstate 15:

• Approximately 30 miles northeast of
Barstow
(just west of Afton Canyon)
• Approximately 20 miles northeast of
Baker (just west of Cima Road)

CHAPTER TWO

Interstate 40

WHILE INTERSTATE 15 OFFERS any number of interesting sites and tourist attractions, Interstate 40 provides a different type of route. This nearly straight shot from Barstow to Needles leads through a desolate land of mountain ranges and big sky country that is often crisscrossed with vapor trails from the military jets that frequently swoop through the area.

I-40 is the southern access route to the East Mojave. Three roads—Kelbaker, Essex and Goffs —lead north into the desert.

Heading southeast down I-40 from Barstow, you'll soon drive through the United States Marine Corps Logisitics Base, then on past the futuristic Solar One facility, Southern California Edison's solar power plant. The Fort Cady Road exit, about

35 miles from Barstow, is the last place for gas, lodging and food until Ludlow, 27 miles to the east. At Ludlow, gas, lodging and food are available; it's the last service stop on I-40 until Needles, 100 miles away! Be very sure to check your water supply, along with gas and oil levels, before heading east.

Kelbaker Road

Twenty-seven miles east of Ludlow, the Amboy-Kelso exit leads to Kelbaker Road. The mostly paved Kelbaker Road climbs through Granite Pass (elevation 4,024 feet), and down toward Kelso (elevation 2,126 feet).

Essex Road

Forty-eight miles east of Ludlow, Essex Road is the entry point to Providence Mountains State Recreation Area and Mitchell Caverns.

Essex Road is a convenient entrance point for traveling to the popular campgrounds at Hole-in-the-Wall and Mid Hills, easily reached from Black Canyon Road, just off Essex Road.

The aptly named Needles—distinctive spiked mountains east of the town.

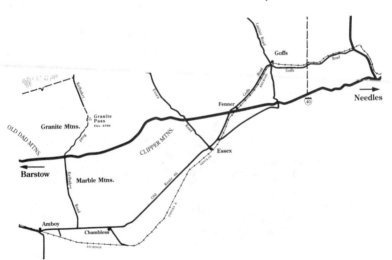

Goffs Road

Fifty-five miles east of Ludlow, Goffs Road leads to the small town of Goffs, and on to Lanfair/Ivanpah Road which leads to the heart of the mining sites in the East Mojave.

Goffs Road also provides the most direct access to Fort Piute to the east.

Goffs, once a steam locomotive watering stop, is now home to fewer than two dozen people. At the Goffs General Store and Country Kitchen, limited supplies—including ice—and short-order meals can be purchased. The store, with its pot-bellied stove and friendly atmosphere, is a social center of sorts, of the East Mojave.

In *The Thousand-Mile Summer,* Colin Fletcher wrote: "In the last rays of the setting sun, the cluster of buildings that was Goffs did not look the sort of place to be unduly worried by automobiles. Or for that matter, to be worried by anything much."

Needles

Named for the spikey mountains to the east of town, Needles is situated just west of the Colorado River. Services, accommodations and supplies are available.

Campgrounds off Interstate 40

Desert Drifter RV Park
Take Daggett exit off I-40
34805 Yermo-Daggett Rd.,
Daggett, CA 92327
(619) 254-3200
80 tent and RV spaces

The Dellwood Travelers Motel & Campground
Take Fort Cady exit, then 1/4 mi. west
        on National Trails (old Rt. 66)
47800 National Trails
Newberry Springs, CA 92365
(619) 257-3348
18 tent and RV spaces

Needles KOA
1 1/2 miles northwest of Needles on
        National Trails Highway
(619) 326-4207
88 tent and RV spaces

Train stations once linked the small towns of the desert, serving as social and transportation centers

U.S. Highway 95

This north-south route, to the east of the desert, is the main road to Searchlight (Nev.), and on to Las Vegas. There are services in the town of Cal-Nev-Ari. A point of interest along the route is at Ibis, site of the desert military war game maneuvers led by General George S. Patton in 1942. A historic marker commemorates the site about 5 miles north of I-40.

One interesting "backdoor" route into the East Mojave is Highway 164 which leads west into California and the tiny town of Nipton. The highway climbs over the McCullough Range and descends to an impressive Joshua tree high plain.

Billboard,
circa 1917

CHAPTER THREE

Route 66

No OTHER ROAD in all of America has inspired more dreams than Route 66. The 2,200-mile asphalt ribbon once stretched from Chicago to Los Angeles and set free the imagination of dreamers all over the nation. It opened up the modern-way west to California.

But most of those who journeyed west on Route 66, Dust Bowl migrants, first-generation children of immigrant parents, wanderers, drifters and vacationers, were frightened by the prospect of crossing the Mojave Desert. In the 1946 volume, *A Guide Book to Highway 66* by Jack D. Rittenhouse, the author observed, "You won't find any desert stretches which are blistered with unendurable heat. Worst stretch is the Mojave Desert, 200 miles of territory running west from the California-Arizona line. . . . To many easterners, the desert is a terrifying thing, but to many who frequent the region the desert is a thing of majestic beauty." In *The Grapes of Wrath*, John Steinbeck wrote, "And 66 goes on over the terrible desert, where the distance shimmers and the black cinder mountains hang unbearably in the distance."

The stretch of Route 66 from just outside Barstow to just west of Needles is the longest stretch of the historic route in California. "How far between towns?" wrote Steinbeck, "It is a terror between towns." It's hardly a terror today, and it's well worth getting off the high-speed interstate to drive through what used to be known as "America's Main Street."

Route 66: America's "Mother Road"

Telephone lines, poles topped with glass insulators, parallel the highway, a reminder of why the route was once termed "the Wire Road." Mountain ranges appear far in the distance; abandoned gas stations, diners and motels dot the route. The tiny settlements that sprang up along this route did so primarily to serve the needs of the travelers that

West-bound travelers often abandoned their autos and took up residence in the desert towns where the breakdowns occurred.

came through. Rittenhouse wrote, "Except for Ludlow, no 'towns' worthy of the name existed between Needles and Daggett, California, a stretch of 150 miles."

Route 66 is still within sight of the interstate from Newberry Springs to Ludlow, but as you travel east through Ludlow, Amboy, Cadiz, Danby, Essex and Fenner—all just off the highway—the trip down Route 66 becomes a journey into America's past.

Ludlow is a good supply point, as described earlier in this guide. About 28 miles east of Ludlow, you'll notice extensive Hawaiian-like lava fields. Amboy Crater, the cause of this flow, lies just south of the road.

Bright, kitchy bright road signs designed to attract maximum attention were common sights along Route 66.

"Route 66 . . . the path of people in flight," wrote John Steinbeck. The road appears unchanged from those earlier days of desert travel.

The town of Amboy, about 5 miles east of the crater, has never consisted of much more than a cafe or two and a motel. A huge sign announces "Roy's Motel and Cafe." Built in the mid-40s, the stop has always been a popular one with tourists. Gas is still available here. About 2 1/2 miles east of town, Kelbaker Road extends south to Route 66; take it for access to Kelso and the East Mojave.

Between Amboy and Essex, you'll notice abandoned autos, closed-down diners and service stations. The buildings may still stand, but the spirit and life behind them appears to have just dried up and blown away—exactly what happened when 66 was bypassed by the interstate.

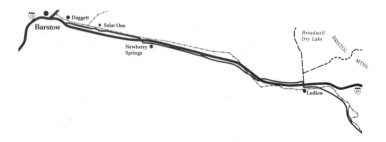

Before the 1987 release of the movie "Bagdad Cafe," the former town of Bagdad had one claim to fame: the longest recorded period of not even a drop of precipitation in 767 days from 1909 to 1912.

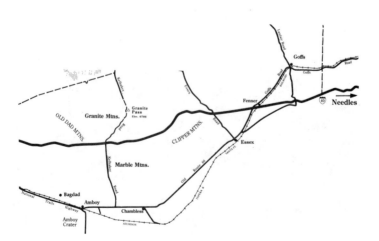

Essex, about 25 miles east of Amboy, has a cafe, a small store and a post office. Essex Road leads to the Providence Mountains and Mitchell Caverns.

Route 66 continues another 13 miles past Essex to Mountain Springs Summit where it rejoins I-40.

The Route 66 trip takes longer than the I-40 route. But, because it offers a unique view of days gone by, take the time. Pull over, get out of the car, sit by the side of the road, and listen to the quiet. It's an eardrum-pounding quiet that cannot usually be perceived. Take in the sight of the barren land, the many mountain ranges, the alien volcanic territory near Amboy Crater. Allow yourself to feel the eternal, unchanged quality of this land. This desolate stretch of highway gives no hint of the metropolis just 200 miles to the west, but it's easy to imagine both the fears and the hopes of the countless travelers who once journeyed across this road, dreaming of a better life.

In the days before fast food, diners and cafes filled the bill. They were places where travelers could get a cheap hot meal, exchange road information, chat and relax before hitting the long highway once again.

CHAPTER FOUR

Other Roads to Adventure: Mojave Road

Neither gloom nor dark of night—or lack of decent roads— could keep these dedicated desert mail carriers from the swift (and dusty) completion of their appointed rounds.

CHALLENGING THE FOUR-WHEEL DRIVE enthusiast is the Mojave Road, a 140-mile-long route that visits many of the most scenic areas in the East Mojave. The rough dirt road was reconstructed and is now maintained by the Friends of the Mojave Road.

The road uses the historic trade route followed by Native Americans as they crossed the desert on their way to the coast. Spanish and Western explorers, miners and mail carriers used the route; eventually settlements and military outposts were established along the road. Today, the Mojave Road stretches from the Fort Mojave Indian Reservation on the Colorado River, west to the former military outpost at Camp Cady.

Along the way, it passes through or near some of the East Mojave's most memorable places, including Fort Piute, Mid Hills, Cinder Cones, Soda Dry Lake and Afton Canyon.

Traveling along the Mojave Road provides access to the heart of the East Mojave, and an experience of the land that is not possible to gain if the visitor only stays on major roads.

The route is marked with cairns (piles of rocks), but your best guide is the *Mojave Road Guide*, written by Dennis Casebier and the Friends of the Mojave Road.

The Mojave Road is a rugged route through desert wilderness. Driving on it requires planning, desert driving experience and appropriately equipped vehicles. It should never be attempted without a group of fellow travelers. Mountain bikers have ridden parts of the Road, and hikers have walked on it, but the Mojave Road is primarily a route to be explored in a four-wheel drive Jeep or similar vehicle.

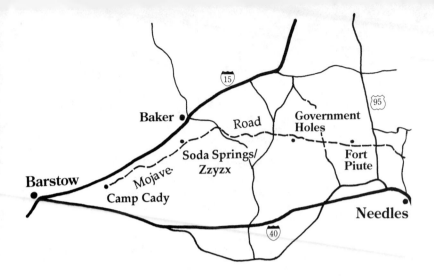

East Mojave Heritage Trail

The 660-mile long East Mojave Heritage Trail is an interpreted four-wheel drive trail that circles the desert. The route, which begins and ends in Needles, tours historic mining areas, travels along railroad routes and passes through some of the most fascinating landscapes of the East Mojave.

Unlike the Mojave Road, which has for centuries been a travel route, the Heritage Trail was established relatively recently. The trail links existing routes of travel; no new routes were developed. Heritage Trail is maintained by the California Association of 4-Wheel Drive Clubs, Inc. Like the Mojave Road, it's best explored in the company of fellow four-wheel drive enthusiasts.

The trail, laid out in four sections, uses old mining roads, abandoned railroad berms, wagon trails, utility line roads, and even a section of old Route 66. Where the Heritage Trail crosses those lands designated as wilderness, travel is prohibited.

Back Country Byways

Soon after Wild Horse Canyon Byway was designated, seven more Back Country Byways were added to the East Mojave Desert: Kelbaker Road, Kelso-Cima Road, Black Canyon Road, Cima Road, Ivanpah-Lanfair Road, Essex Road, and Cedar Canyon Road.

The East Mojave's eight-byway system totals a somewhat astonishing 222 miles—the most extensive system in the West. The roads crisscross the desert and lead to, or close to, most of the major scenic attractions.

All the desert byways are classified Type I, with the exception of Type II Wild Horse Canyon Byway. Type I byways are paved or have an all-weather surface, and can be negotiated by passengers cars. (Other classifications: Type II roads are unpaved, with high-clearance vehicles or four-wheel drive recommended; Type III byways are very rough roads, even tracks, requiring four-wheel drive; Type IV byways are trails for mountain bike, snowmobile or ATV use.)

The byways, covered in detail in the touring chapters of this guide, are a great way to see the land. All the roads declared "Back Country Byways" certainly deserve the designation. As you explore deeper and deeper in the heart of the desert, you'll probably want to nominate a few of your favorite remote roads for this honor.

The Mojave Road attracts desert drivers who love the desert's wide-open spaces.

Scenic Wild Horse Canyon Road from Mid Hills to Hole-in-the-Wall: America's first Back Country Byway.

Desert crossings weren't always made in air-conditioned comfort. Past desert travelers crossed on foot or horseback, or in a jolting, creaky horse-drawn wagon.

CHAPTER FIVE

Desert Travel

MANY NOTABLE TRAVELERS have journeyed through the hot white heart of the Mojave since Father Francisco Garces first passed this way in 1776. Other early Mojave explorers include Jedediah Smith, Kit Carson, and John C. Frémont. They had little idea of what to expect during their desert crossing. Traveling without detailed maps, high-tech equipment, or freeze-dried foods, they still managed to make the overland trek toward the coast.

Today, we enjoy the benefit of all sorts of undreamed-of modern accoutrements, making desert journeys more comfortable than they were in days past. But the most important aids to desert travel remain as simple as they were 200 years ago—common sense, advance planning and packing the right supplies.

Planning Ahead

Individuals accustomed to spending their days in air-conditioned comfort are in for a surprise when they venture into the desert. It's a harsh environment that demands adaptation by inhabitants and visitors alike. Daily extremes of hot and cold are the norm; a 100-degree day can become a 50-degree night. It's important to be prepared—not simply for comfort, but for survival.

The unforgiving desert does not allow visitors to make many mistakes. Those ill-prepared may be unable to deal with threatening situations. Desert dangers are real, and using common sense is essential.

Planning ahead is the first rule of desert travel. Study maps and know where you're going. Become informed about weather patterns, and know what temperatures and climatic conditions to expect. Use this information to plan your trip.

As you study your maps, determine where to obtain services—food, water, gas, ice, etc. Anticipate when you'll need to replenish fuel and supplies, and purchase them whenever you have the chance, since gas stations and stores are few in the East Mojave.

Before you depart on a desert journey, leave a detailed itinerary with a friend or family member. Be sure to indicate when you expect to return; call later if your plans change.

The Goffs Store sells as much as a ton of ice a month—mostly in small sacks.

When You're There

Don't miss the chance to stock up on incidental supplies whenever you can. Stores at Cima, Goffs and Nipton, along with the Newberry Market and the Sunshine Store, are among the few desert outposts.

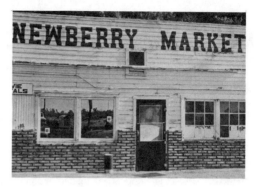

Pay attention to your physical responses in the desert. Temperature extremes and dryness make it a stressful environment. If you're overweight or out-of-shape, take it easy, and don't push yourself to keep up with your fitter friends.

Although it's quite tempting, don't overschedule. There are so many places to explore in the East Mojave that you could spend a lifetime and never see them! A million-and-a-half acres is lot of land; planning a weekend whirlwind trip is likely to leave you feeling frustrated and exhausted. Pick one or two areas to explore during each trip, and plan to return again.

Hiking during the warmer months is best done in the early morning or late afternoon hours. During the heat of the day, try to find a place in some shade, and catch up on your reading, write in your journal, take a nap or enjoy a conversation with friends. It's not the time to be out on a strenuous hike.

Water

Water is the essential life-sustaining substance in the desert. It's in short supply in this arid environment, and most natural water sources are probably unsafe to drink. Therefore, it's imperative that desert travelers be prepared at all times with sufficient quantities of water. An absolute minimum to carry is one gallon per person per day. Remember that a gallon of water weighs about eight pounds.

Anytime you venture out into the desert on foot, for even a short period, bring a bottle of water. Plastic bottles sold in backpacking and outdoors shops are convenient and easy to carry. It's far better to carry water and not need it, than to be stuck in an isolated area without a canteen. Bring enough water for each member in your party.

The key to staying properly hydrated outdoors is to drink before you become thirsty; take a few sips every 10 to 15 minutes or so. Don't ration your water, and don't waste it.

Fill up when you have the opportunity (at campgrounds and at roadside rest stops; purchase water at stores when you can); it's a good idea to have more than you think you'll need.

The romantic notion of finding a huge barrel cactus with plenty of stored water in it is highly unlikely in the East Mojave.

Food

DESERT SURVIVAL

Protein foods use more water for digestion than do carbohydrates; avoid meat, cheese, and peanut butter. Use dates, raisins, fruit or honey.

When packing food for desert travel, consider the dry climate, heat and cold you'll encounter. Additionally, consider nutritional requirements, tastes and appetite. Leave the junk, the sugary "treats" and empty calories at home. Better yet, leave them in the store, and choose instead healthy, high-quality fuel foods that are simple to pack and transport and easy to prepare.

You needn't go the dehydrated food route unless you're planning a backpacking trip where weight is a major concern.

Pack plenty of trail mix, dried and fresh fruit, cut-up vegetables, whole-grain crackers and low-sugar cookies for trail snacks and light lunches. Cereal straight from the box, peanut butter sandwiches and other simple foods are camp staples. Boxes of juice pack and travel well. Remember that foods—especially bread, bagels and rolls—dry out quickly in the arid desert environment. Always wrap foods well before storing them.

If you bring a cooler and a stove, your food options increase dramatically. And if you are fortunate enough to have a willing camp cook in your party, you may be treated to the indescribable treat of scrambled eggs, hot coffee or chili prepared outdoors. Tantalizing as the thought may be, remember that you must use a stove or campground fire pits and grills. Bring your own fuel, charcoal or wood—do not gather wood in the desert.

Always pack and carry some food with you when you venture out into the desert.

Clothing

Heat, cold, wind and rain, cactus and rugged terrain characteristic of the desert combine to make proper dressing essential for protection and comfort.

Pack simple, sturdy clothing that doesn't show the dirt. Natural fabrics, especially cotton and wool, are favorite choices because of their breathability and durability.

The simplest approach to desert dressing is to layer your clothing, adding to or subtracting from the layers as the temperature and wind allow. Make sure you choose roomy, comfortable clothing that doesn't bind anywhere. Classic long-sleeved button-front shirts and sweaters, T-shirts and tank tops are all smart choices, as are jeans and khakis. In general, long pants are preferred in the desert for the protection they offer from cactus and the sun, but long socks and hiking shorts may be more comfortable. Sweats are comfortable and warm in the early morning and evening hours.

What you wear on your extremities is as important as your body wear. In warm weather, head protection is a must. Popular choices include baseball caps, broad-brimmed canvas or straw hats. In cold weather, however, a knitted watch cap is best for keeping in your body heat; mittens or gloves make winter desert trekking more pleasant.

Selecting the proper footwear is always a question for outdoor adventurers. Desert hiking requires more substantial footwear than a pair of lightweight running shoes. The terrain is rough, and the temperature of the sand can really heat up during the day, making even short hikes literally a blistering experience. Sturdy hiking boots or the hiking shoes manufactured by running-shoe companies are good choices. Since waterproof materials are rarely required for desert hiking, the fabric-

Whether hiking down a desert trail or scrambling up rock walls what every well dressed hiker should wear: loose, lightweight, comfortable clothing, sturdy hiking shoes and a hat for protection from the sun.

and-leather construction of these running shoe-hiking boot hybrids is ideal. These lightweight boots breathe, and can be much more comfortable than heavy-duty waffle stompers. Look for long-wearing soles and stiff shanks for comfort and support.

Pack running shoes or other comfortable footwear to wear around camp.

Above all, when selecting footwear, get a proper fit. Improperly fitting boots or shoes will never be comfortable. Period.

Outerwear is largely a matter of personal choice. Synthetics such as Synchilla, Gore-Tex, Polarplus and Thermax have been fashioned into jackets, pullovers and pants. They offer maximum protection from the elements, with minimal weight or bulk. Down jackets and vests are also popular and comfortable for cool weather or nighttime desert wear. Windbreakers offer inexpensive protection from the almost ever-present winds in the East Mojave; they are easily stuffed into a day pack or fanny pack.

Many desert rats swear that their most valuable piece of clothing is a bandanna. These brightly colored squares of cloth can serve as a handkerchief, neckerchief, towel, washcloth, headband, loincloth, bikini top, sweatband, head scarf, tablecloth, napkin—well, the list is limited only by your imagination. . . .

Gear

• **Maps** Because the East Mojave covers such a vast territory, a good map is indispensible. The Auto Club's San Bernardino County map is useful for getting to the East Mojave.

—The USGS Topo maps cover most of the area, but since the East Mojave sprawls over more than a dozen maps, they tend to be inconvenient.

—The BLM offers a series of California desert maps. The Providence Mountains and New York Mountains maps in this series are helpful, but they don't cover the entire desert.

• **Flashlight** Depending on your habits, pack anything from a mini penlight to a large model complete with emergency flasher. Camp or candle lanterns are helpful, especially during the winter when days are short and nights are (very) long. Bring extra batteries, bulb and candles.

• **Compass** The indispensable tool for geographical orientation. If you know how to use it, bring a compass. If you don't know how to use one, learn how; outdoors shops and many organizations frequently offer map and compass classes.

• **Sunglasses** They protect from the intense light, glare and wind so characteristic of the East Mojave. Polarized lenses and UV ratings between 50 and 80 ensure real protection, not just stylish looks. Attach a leash to your glasses for convenience.

• **Pocketknife** What comes in handy more frequently than a trusty Swiss Army knife? Enough said.

• **Emergency Supplies** Extra food and water, which you may wish to keep in your vehicle all the time. Waterproof matches, fire-starting tablets, a well-stocked first-aid kit and a couple of blankets. Replenish as needed. One of the best ways to be prepared in a medical emergency is to have taken a Red Cross CPR class.

• **Toilet paper and tissues**

• **Sunscreen** Get the SPF rating that's right for you, and use it. Reapply frequently.

• **Lip balm** To protect from chapped lips, look for one containing a sunscreen for best protection.

• **Skin lotion** To counteract the drying effects of the desert.

• **Camera** Always bring more film than you think you'll need, along with an extra battery.

• **Insect repellant** Keeps the critters off you.

• **Sewing kit** Buttons pop off when you least expect it.

• **Notebook or journal and pen** A good place to scribble your thoughts and take notes about your observations in the East Mojave.

• **Daypack or fanny pack** Easy to carry on a day hike; keep an extra water bottle in each for convenience.

• **Binoculars for bird-watching**

• **Telescope for sky-watching**

• **Any prescribed medications**

• **And always, a good book** As you read through this guide, you'll notice quotes from some favorite desert classics.

Don't forget to phone home, even in "the middle of nowhere."

61

CHAPTER SIX

Desert Driving

A 1911 Stanley Steamer—durable enough for desert travel, even when loaded with family and friends.

BECAUSE THERE ARE SO few amenities available in the East Mojave, you must not only bring your own supplies, but consider your automobile a self-contained "survival module." Be certain that your vehicle is road-worthy and capable of withstanding harsh desert conditions. In case of emergency, your life could literally depend on it.

The image of bouncing across the desert in a dilapidated old jalopy may have some romantic appeal; it symbolizes the highly cherished notion of the freedom of the open road. In reality, however, driving a well-maintained, comfortable and reliable vehicle provides a sense of confidence and security—and a real measure of safety as well.

Naturalist Joseph Wood Krutch described venturing into the desert as "rewarding travel in an unfrequented land." Travel in the desert is rewarding for a number of reasons, not the least of which is the fact that it truly is an "unfrequented land." The wide-open spaces and lonely desert roads are particularly appealing to those seeking the solitude and quiet the desert offers.

The shimmering asphalt ribbon of Highway 164, also known as Nipton Road, heads east to Searchlight, Nevada. An impressive Joshua tree forest lines the highway east of the border.

But in an unexpected situation, such as a vehicle breakdown, that feeling of peaceful solitude can quickly become a fearful experience in a hostile environment. Therefore, driving a road-worthy vehicle is of utmost importance in the desert.

The East Mojave is bounded by two major highways. Since the area is fairly isolated from cities, it's probable that any vehicle that's driven the one hundred-plus miles it takes to get there is in pretty good shape. But venturing into the desert, far from highway services, requires some special preparation.

The perils of desert driving include extreme heat and glare (especially when driving east in the morning or west in the afternoon); winter cold, ice and snow. The long, straight roads can become monotonous and sleep-inducing day or night. Dirt roads require special driving skills, and the unfamiliar territory demands navigational expertise. Weather conditions, including dust, wind and thunderstorms which can cause flash floods, are other difficulties faced by desert drivers.

Not even the early AAA touring bureau drivers, responsible for mapping and assisting fellow travelers, were exempt from getting stuck in the sand.

Your vehicle is a home away from home— keep it well-stocked and well-maintained.

A Historical Perspective

In the early days of automobile travel in the desert, none of the roads were paved. Little more than trails—sometimes marked with signposts—the roads gave drivers a real adventurous ride through the desert. The earliest autos weren't even equipped with tops or windshields, and electric lighting systems did not come into use until 1912. Still, intrepid individuals made their way to the Mojave for spirited travel experience.

Over the years, travelers have been advised to carry equipment and supplies to cope with emergencies. Earliest autos were notoriously unreliable; a 1914-1917 Auto Club checklist suggested the following:

- two stout pieces of rope, each 10 feet long
- a collapsible bucket for radiator water
- two wide canvas strips, each about 100 feet long, sewn together (for getting unstuck)
- a can, funnel and chamois filter
- 5-gallon water and gas cans filled, plus 2 to 3 desert water bags
- a tire repair kit, including pump, vulcanizer, tube liners and sleeves, casing repair stock, friction tape
- a box of repair parts, contents depended on the make, model and reputation for reliability of the vehicle
- a tour book, available maps and a good compass
- a luggage carrier for food and personal gear

In the 1946 book, A *Guidebook to Route 66* by Jack Rittenhouse, the author offered "A few small tips which mean big comforts: DON'T WORRY! A trip is no fun if worry sits at the wheel, even if this worry is not voiced to others in the car. So—first of all—rest assured that you're not going to be 'hung up' in some forsaken spot. You'll never be more than a score of miles from gas, even in the most desolate areas. There are no impossible grades."

Equipment Checklist

Although today's better maintained, more reliable vehicles may not be as prone to breakdown as those in the past, many of the precautions suggested over the years still apply today. An up-to-date checklist includes the following:

- a well-maintained vehicle
- recent oil change
- recent tune-up
- good battery
- good starter
- check all fluid levels: water, coolant, oil, etc.
- check all belts; carry a spare fan belt
- check tires, carry a good spare, jack and tools
- check suspension
- check windshield wiper blades
- carry repair manual, extra water and coolant for the vehicle; if you carry extra gasoline make sure it's in a proper container
- carry flares, fuses, blankets, extra food and water, tools and an up-to-date automobile club membership

Map Reading

A turn-of-the-century U.S. Geological Survey report noted, "With some persons, the faculty of getting lost amounts to genius. They are able to accomplish it wherever they are. The only suitable advice for them is to keep out of the desert. There are safer places in which to exercise their talent." If those words strike home, remember that map-reading is a skill. And like any other skill, performance improves with practice.

Certainly there is nothing more nerve-wracking or upsetting than the experience of a frustrated driver demanding directions from an unsure navigator. Not only is it frustrating, but potentially hazardous, especially when intensified by traffic, hot weather, fatigue or confusing territory.

To avoid such disorienting and upsetting scenarios, spend time before departure planning and mapping out excursions. Write down directions, road names and number and pertinent landmarks to prevent on-the-road confusion. While the main access roads to the East Mojave are well-marked, many lesser roads are not signed at all. Therefore, pay close attention to mileage on the odometer when following directions to locations throughout the desert.

A jumble of street signs can be confusing to even the most seasoned traveler. Plan out your trip on the map before venturing out on the road.

Road Conditions in the East Mojave

The main roads in the East Mojave—Essex, Kelbaker and Kelso-Cima—are paved. Many other main roads, however—Ivanpah and Cedar Canyon—are not. They are graded, and usually easily passable by the typical sedan. Other lesser roads in the desert are gravel, unmaintained dirt that can become very soft and rutted, or passable by four-wheel drive only. Therefore, the driver's experience and the type of vehicle must be considered carefully when mapping a route and choosing roads.

It's not unusual to encounter even a reclusive wild burro on the sandy backroads of the East Mojave.

Desert Driving Tips

• Contact the Desert Information Center in Barstow, or your local Automobile Club office, to check current road conditions and discuss your proposed route if you intend to drive on graded or dirt roads.

• Keep tires at normal pressure; underinflation wears on them and can cause blowouts

• Make sure vehicle has proper clearance for the road surface

• Drive slowly and carefully on dirt roads

• Drive only on established roads —no cross-country driving

• Shift to lower gears on grades

• Pay attention to temperature gauges—air conditioning is more comfortable, but it is taxing on the engine—if the engine heats up, turn off the air conditioning

• If you get stuck in soft dirt or sand, remain calm; try backing up, then carefully shift into low and back to reverse. Be careful not to attempt this for an extended period of time; it's easy to burn up a transmission with this maneuver. If there's no other way, dig, push or tow the vehicle to safer ground.

• In case of breakdown, stay with your car—it offers more protection than wandering in the desert unprotected from the harsh environment

• Stay out of washes, expecially during rain or thunderstorms

• Do not travel alone

Keep in mind, as you drive through the desert, to take it easy. Don't try to drive too far, too fast or too long. If you get tired, pull over and rest or switch drivers for awhile. If you become disoriented, stop, regroup, consult the maps and examine landmarks to become re-oriented once again.

In 1937, photographer Edward Weston traveled extensively throughout the West. His wife Charis kept a journal, and her observations make it clear that while the vehicles have changed, driving in the desert hasn't really changed in more than fifty years. "Luckily traffic was not heavy—each of the two cars we did meet left powdery dust sifting down on us for ten minutes after."

Outdoor lovers agree that it's impossible to know the land unless you venture off the highway and explore it. Nowhere is that more true than in the East Mojave. Only after you leave the main roads that bound the "lonesome triangle" can the appeal of the place become clear. It seems to speak to the all-American pioneer spirit that lives on to this day.

Know your limits—and those of your vehicle—and don't push them, or this could happen to you.

PART II

Getting
To
Know
The Land

The desert is the opposite of all that we naturally find pleasing. Yet I believe that its hold upon those who have once fallen under its spell is deeper and more enduring than is the charm of forest or sea or mountain.

—Joseph Smeaton Chase

CHAPTER SEVEN

The Land

THE MOJAVE IS FAR from the world's largest or most severe desert, but it's surely one of the most geologically fascinating. Geologists like this desert because the land is naked, exposed. Recorded in the ancient rocks and vast sands is the history of the world.

The 54,000-square-mile Mojave is the smallest of the four North American deserts. It's situated south of the Great Basin, north of the Sonoran, and northwest of the Chihuahuan. Its elevation ranges primarily from 2,000 to 4,000 feet, although it includes both the lowest point in the United States, at Badwater in Death Valley (282 feet below sea level) and many mountain peaks above 5,000 feet. Southern Californians often call it "the high desert" because of its elevation.

The topography of the Mojave is termed "basin and range." It is characterized by south-trending mountain ranges rising abruptly from the desert floor, separated by irregularly spaced basins. (Basins, unlike valleys, are not drained by rivers.) The mountains have been formed by the movement of the land along earthquake faults that run through here.

While deserts can be hot or cold (the frozen Arctic is considered a desert), the common factor among all of them is dryness. Technically, a desert is a land that receives less than ten inches of precipitation annually; its evaporation rate usually exceeds the amount of precipitation. The Mojave averages less than six inches of precipitation, most of which occurs during the winter months, often in the form of snowfall.

Temperature extremes are characteristic of deserts—not only from summer to winter, but from day to night. During the summer, it's not uncommon for the temperature to fluctuate fifty degrees in twenty-four hours. During the day, the surface of the soil absorbs most of the incoming solar radiation because there is so little humidity and so little vegetation to deflect it. At night, the heat is rapidly lost as it's re-radiated back to the sky.

The mountain ranges to the west and south of the Mojave are responsible for the dryness of the desert. As warm, moist ocean air cools, it rises up the slopes of the Tehachapi, San Gabriel, San Bernardino and San Jacinto ranges, and dumps rain and snow on the western slopes. As the air flows down the east side, it becomes warmer and drier. Deserts situated on the east side of coastal mountains are termed "rainshadow deserts."

The mountains also cause the ever-present afternoon winds in the Mojave. Air movement occurs to equalize temperature difference between the mountains and the comparatively warmer desert floor. These winds tend to dissipate by nightfall, but not before they dry the air and erode the surfaces of the land, distributing natural materials and debris in their wake.

Classic basin and range formations, typical of the Mojave.

The Mojave—East and West

The West Mojave is that part of the desert bounded on the east by the Mojave River. It sweeps north and west from Barstow toward Death Valley and the southern Sierra Nevada.

The West Mojave takes in the burgeoning Antelope Valley, including Lancaster and Victorville. The East is the larger part of the Mojave and extends east to the Nevada border and to the Colorado River.

Topographically, the East and West Mojave are quite different. The West presents great sandscapes, with many flat areas and some isolated ridges and buttes. The East Mojave, too, has its flatlands—primarily in the form of big basins and wide valleys between mountain ranges, but it is the mountain ranges themselves that differentiate the East Mojave from other desert lands.

The East Mojave represents a time scale almost beyond human comprehension. From the granite formations of Mesozoic Age—more than 150 million years old—to young 10 million year old Cenozoic rocks, the igneous, metamorphic and sedimentary rocks reveal a long and complex past.

During more recent geological time, some 20,000 years ago, this land was covered with abundant waters, rivers and lakes. Marshlands, grassy valleys and stands of pines, junipers and oaks sheltered a wide array of mammals and birds. Fossil remains of extinct sloth, camels, bison and enormous prehistoric horses are evidence of a very different land than we see here today.

But approximately 11,000 years ago, the weather became drier and warmer; as the lakes dried up, the forests and grasslands shriveled away and died. With their food supply depleted, many of the animals also perished. Indians seeking available food and water migrated throughout the area. In true Darwinian fashion, all life in the rapidly growing desert became a matter of survival of the fittest.

As life forms have changed over the ages, so too, has the land. Hot, dry winds have eroded mountains into grains of sand, then built them up again as sand dunes. Runoff from irregular, but violent thunderstorms has carved canyons and washes; debris carried down from the mountains by the turgid waters has built up fanlike formations. Volcanic activity has created cinder cones, spectacular rock formations and lava flows, and geologic movement along faults has crumpled, folded and tipped this stratified land. These natural forces have created dramatic geographic features, unique in all the world.

Mountains

It's often said that the East Mojave is a desert of mountains. These mountains are situated along north-south trending faults. A glance at a map indicates chains of mountain ranges throughout the area. Especially prominent is the southwest-northeast trending chain formed by the Granite, Providence, Mid Hill and New York ranges.

Ranging from southeast to northwest are the Sacramento, Bristol and Old Dad Mountain ranges; ranging from north to south are the Piutes and Ivanpahs.

The rugged granitic ranges of the East Mojave have been highly eroded; characteristic of this action is the build-up of loose sedimentary materials at the base of the mountains.

These apron-shaped formations are called alluvial fans. When alluvial fans grow so large that they begin to converge and fill in the distance between them, they are called bajadas.

Cholla gardens and table top mountains, combined with clear skies and fluffy clouds— just another day in the scenic East Mojave.

The lunar-like landscape of the Cinder Cone area—a National Natural Landmark.

Volcanic Formations

Located in the northwest section of the desert is the 25,600-acre area known as the "Cinder Cones National Natural Landmark." The 32 conical-shaped cinder cone formations that comprise this landmark are actually extinct volcanoes. Some were formed fairly recently—within the last 1,000 years—while others date back nearly 10 million years. Black basalt, material thrown out by the erupting cones, has built up a thick layer on an underlying granite base.

East of the cinder cones is the 75-square-mile formation known as Cima Dome. While not technically a volcanic formation, Cima Dome is the result of a huge uplift of molten rock. It's been eroded over the years, and today appears as an almost-perfectly symmetrical granite formation that rises gently above the surrounding area.

Castle Peaks—jagged, red-colored, spire-like formations that rise steeply from the surrounding New York Mountains—are volcanic in nature. The mysterious towers near Hole-in-the-Wall campground, along with the Swiss-cheese-shaped rocks in nearby Banshee Canyon, are other examples of vulcanism in the East Mojave.

Basin, Range and More

Dry lake beds, or playas, are characteristic of basin and range lands. Remnants of lakes that evaporated long ago, these flat areas are highly alkaline, and support few forms of life. Soda Dry Lake, located on the western boundary of the East Mojave, is a very large playa that can become wet when rainfall is significant.

Dry washes, also called arroyos, are cut by water scouring the desert floor. They look like dry streambeds, but they can rapidly become raging waterways—flash floods—during thunderstorms or significant rainfalls. Although it may seem that the wind is the dominant cause of erosion in the desert, the presence of water—occasional though it may be— actually sculpts and carves the land to a more significant degree. Flash floods can swiftly carry rocks, boulders, branches, sand and silt, depositing the materials far from where they were originally picked up by the rushing waters.

Some 26 mountain ranges throughout the East Mojave provide dramatic views in every direction.

Desert varnish, a distinctive, shiny, dark-brown coating that appears on rocks, occurs when manganese and iron are present; it may also be related to the presence of acids that occur during the decomposition of lichen.

Desert pavement, also called desert mosaic, is the cemented-together surface of closely fitted rocks, pebbles and gravel and other materials. This hard, flat surface is created by a combination of wind and rain moving the small rocks, and flushing away the fine soil.

Tabletop mesas occur throughout the East Mojave, the most distinctive of which is known as Table Mountain, a 6,176-foot mesa.

Of all the distinctive natural features in the desert, perhaps none is more deeply moving than the special quality of the light, the vastness of the sky. Poets and writers have long recorded the magnificence of the opalescent light, the spectacular sunrises and sunsets. For city dwellers all too accustomed to viewing murky night skies, gazing at the Milky Way on display is a revelation and a truly awesome experience. This is a place where shooting stars and constellations appear with startling clarity. Study your sky charts and bring your telescopes; the night sky is as dramatic here as it gets.

CHAPTER EIGHT

Plants & Animals

IN HIS CLASSIC turn-of-the-century book, *The Desert*, John C. Van Dyke wrote, "Nature does not bend the elements to favor the plants and animals; she makes the plants and the animals do the bending." Life in the desert requires adapation, not only for visitors, but for wildlife.

Successful desert plants and animals have adjusted to conditions that seem designed to forbid any form of life. Unique, specifically adapted plants and animals have developed in spite of temperature extremes, intense sunlight, fierce and frequent winds, and long periods of drought.

Most people think of deserts as barren wastelands, devoid of life except for a cactus or two. But most desert areas support diverse populations of plants and animals. The varied landforms and range of altitudes in the East Mojave, and the localized presence of water, create a number of specific ecological communities.

The East Mojave Desert is an exciting place for botanists and biologists because the area is so vast and uncharted and because of the possibility of discovering new life forms. Two University of Califonia herpetologists recently discovered a new species of western toad. New species of Jerusalem cricket have turned up in the sand dunes.

Enthusiasm in the scientific community is tempered with worry about the effects of human intrusion into the desert world. Gone from the Mojave, from the earth, is the Tecopa pupfish, the Mojave tarplant and more. Researchers say we don't know enough about the desert to know what is being lost.

"We don't know that much about the desert, and we ought to preserve it so future generations have some options," declares Gerald Scherba, a biologist formerly with the Desert Sudies Center in Zzyzx. "Unless you absolutely need a resource, the prudent thing is to leave it alone."

Joshua Tree—
High Desert Woodland

Probably the most distinctive of the Mojave Desert communities, the Joshua tree woodland is found at altitudes from 2,500 to 4,500 feet, on well-drained desert slopes. In the East Mojave, the Joshua tree woodland can be found at Cima Dome, Ivanpah Valley and Lanfair Valley.

The Joshua tree, with its upturned branches is easily recognized but not always admired. Explorer John C. Frémont called it, "the most repulsive tree in the vegetable kingdom." Writer Charles Francis Saunders noted, "The trees themselves were as grotesque as the creations of a bad dream; the shaggy trunks and limbs were twisted and seemed writhing as though in pain, and dagger-pointed leaves were clenched in bristling fists of inhospitality." And Joseph Smeaton Chase, who hardly ever met a tree he didn't like, wrote, "It is a weird, menacing object, more like some conception of Poe's or Doré's than any work of wholesome Mother Nature. One can scarcely find a term of ugliness that is not apt for this plant. A misshapen pirate with belts, boots, hands, and teeth stuck full of daggers is as near as I can come to a human analogy. The wood is a harsh, rasping fibre; knife-blades, long, hard and keen, fill the place of leaves; the flower is greenish white and ill-smelling; and the fruit a cluster of nubbly pods, bitter and useless. A landscape filled with Joshua trees has a nightmare effect even in broad daylight; at the witching hour it can be almost infernal."

Despite the unflattering descriptions, the Joshua tree and surrounding community do have their attractions. The dramatic colors of the sky at sunset provide a breathtaking backdrop for the

John C. Frémont, who regularly encountered Joshua trees as he traveled through the East Mojave, described it as ". . . the most repulsive tree in the vegetable kingdom."

world's largest Joshua tree forest which grows on Cima Dome.

The Joshua tree provides shelter for a number of small desert animals, particularly rodents, such as the kangaroo rat, desert wood rat, and ground squirrel. Birds, including the pinyon jay, logger-head shrike and Scott's oriole, make their nests in the gnarled branches. Reptiles inhabiting the community include the chuckwalla, desert night lizard and desert tortoise. The yucca moth enjoys a sym-biotic relationship with the Joshua tree. The moth fertilizes the trees' flowers by transporting pollen from stamen to pistil; some of the germinated seeds then serve as food for the moth larvae.

Other members of the Joshua tree woodland include: Barrel cactus, chollas, hedgehog cactus, and beavertail cactus, as well as the Mojave yucca, California juniper, Utah juniper, paperbag bush, spiny tetradymia, desert bunch grass, galleta blad-der sage, creosote bush and buckwheat.

Creosote Bush— Low Desert Scrub

This drought-tolerant community is the most common in the East Mojave, found primarily in the low, dry valleys at less than 2,000 or 3,000 feet in elevation. A particularly good example thrives in Wildhorse Canyon, near Hole-in-the-Wall. Most of the creosote bush community consists of widely spaced shrubs which grow three to six feet tall.

The creosote bush, which is the most recognizable plant in this community, is a hardy plant that withstands prolonged periods of drought. The creosote bush is often called "greasewood" for the resinous substance that coats its leaves. The plant has a pungent, distinctive odor; the Spanish word for it, *Hediondilla*, means "little stinker." Although it is a scrubby bush, the creosote has an extensive root system which searches out any available moisture. The creosote bushes growing in Soggy Dry Lake (southwest of the East Mojave), are said to be the the the world's oldest living things. Called King Clone, they are estimated to be more than 10,000 years old.

Also characteristic of this community is the so-called "Devil's Garden," a grouping of several types of cactus interspersed with boulders and other rock formations.

Other members of the community include brittlebush, desert mallow, ocotillo, burrobush, indigo bush, dye bush, desert lily, Bigelow's cholla, silver cholla, teddy bear and buckhorn cholla, and pincushion.

Joseph Smeaton Chase, who disdained cholla as much as he did the Joshua tree, wrote in his classic *California Desert Trails*, "It is an ugly object three of four feet high, with stubby arms standing out like amputated stumps. . . . The Indians say that they jump at you: this sounds like an exaggeration, but upon my word I don't know. Often when I have felt sure that I passed clear of a certain cholla I found he had me after all." Careless or unsuspecting hikers, beware.

Many of the animals that inhabit this community are small, nocturnal rodents which are rarely seen by desert visitors. Instead, the presence of the animals—ground squirrel, jackrabbit, kangaroo rat, and pocket mouse—is indicated by their tracks.

More easily observed species include several birds: the roadrunner, Costa's hummingbird, common raven, cactus wren, black-throated sparrow. Others that might be seen are the zebra-tailed lizard, iguana, and the desert tortoise.

Author Joseph Smeaton Chase (California Desert Trails, *1919) usually had a good word for all desert flora— but not for cholla.*

Hardly a barren land, the East Mojave supports an abundance of diverse life forms.

Desert Dry Woodland

Dry, sandy wash communities are found throughout the East Mojave, wherever water carves its way after a thunderstorm or extended rainy period. Usually found in valleys beneath the mountains, these dry drainage areas quickly fill with an enormous volume of water following storms. These flash floods carry boulders, rocks, shrubs, and any other debris that cross their course.

Desert willows, with their long taproots that seek a permanent water supply, are common along washes. Their pink-lined trumpet-shaped flowers, long pods and slender leaves makes them easily identifiable.

Other plants that grow along drainage washes include mesquite and cat's claw, two related species that bloom with yellow flowers. Desert holly, desert almond and several wildflower species flourish here after winter rains.

Animals include many of the same dwellers found in other desert communities: jackrabbit, desert cottontail, ground squirrel, desert wood rat, cactus mouse, several birds, lizards, sidewinder and desert tortoise.

Pinyon-Juniper Woodland

This community is found in desert mountains between 3,500 and 6,000 feet in elevation. In the East Mojave, pinyon-juniper woodlands can be explored in the New York, Providence and Ivanpah ranges, as well as Clark Mountain.

Higher elevations, cooler temperatures and greater amounts of moisture than occur in low-lying valleys allow the growth of pinyon pine, California and Utah juniper and scrub oak. Other species typically found include black bush, box thorn, Mojave yucca, silver cholla and desert bunch grass

Coyote, jackrabbit, California ground squirrel, pocket gopher and pinon mouse inhabit the woodland community, as do a number of birds, including the woodpecker, pinon jay, rock wren, black-throated gray warbler and gray vireo.

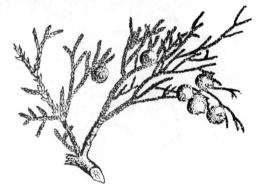

Riparian Woodlands and Marshes

Found along streams such as Piute Creek and along the Mojave River in Afton Canyon and near Camp Cady, this community's year-round water supply supports trees such as cottonwood, willow and mesquite. These native species, however, are threatened by the growth of the nonnative tamarisk, which was introduced to the area from the Mediterranean more than 100 years ago. The invasive tamarisk, also called salt cedar, consumes great amounts of water, and tends to choke out the other trees. Efforts to remove the tamarisk must be very aggressive to be effective; chain saws and strong herbicides are required. Each year volunteer workers spend countless hours clearing riparian areas of the tenacious invader.

Streamside communities frequently attract large bird populations, and the seasonal habitation of migratory species. Many other desert dwellers seek water in riparian communities, most spectacular of which is the bighorn sheep, which are known to frequent Afton Canyon in the dark and quiet hours.

The Desert in Bloom

Wildflower displays are especially delightful in the desert. Brightly colored blossoms contrast vibrantly with the neutral-hued desert environment. But wildflowers bloom only when conditions allow. There must be plenty of evenly spaced winter precipitation, and warmth, but not too much heat in the spring. Kelso Dunes, Ivanpah Valley and the Cadiz Dunes, just south of the East Mojave, are three areas where wildflowers can be expected when the conditions are right.

Coreopsis, encelia, desert primrose, desert verbena and the blooms of the Mohave mound cactus are just a few of the more common East Mojave wildflowers. Many writers and poets have been inspired by the unlikely desert blooms.

The plants and animals of the desert, confronted continually with the harshness of their environment, have made remarkable adaptations in order to survive. Desert visitors can help ensure their survival by enjoying, observing and photographing the numerous species, but not disturbing them in any way.

Animals in the East Mojave

While there are hundreds of animal species in the desert, you're likely to see only a few. You're almost guaranteed to spot jackrabbits and range cattle, ravens and an assortment of lizards and birds; you may even spot a coyote near dusk. But you may travel in this arid land for years before spotting a bighorn sheep or desert tortoise. The animals are there, but they tend to be quite reclusive.

This visitor knows to observe the desert tortoise from a respectful distance. Look, but don't touch.

Bighorn Sheep

They are magnificent creatures, shy and usually hidden from sight. They live primarily on rugged mountain peaks, venturing to lowlands only to water occasionally. The memory of a fleeting glimpse of such an animal will last a lifetime.

The winter of 1988 was the first time in 114 years that hunting of bighorn sheep was authorized and legal in California. The California Department of Fish and Game sold a hunting permit for $100,000 in 1993.

The hunting of these animals has been protested by many, including a group known as "Hunt Saboteurs," who use air horns and other techniques to foil the hunt. On the other side of the issue are hunting enthusiasts and agency officials. They argue that the permit fees help Fish and Game maintain the herds all year long, and that the hunters are allowed to kill only aged animals that would soon die anyway.

Somewhat ironically, the same agency that has authorized hunting of the rare bighorn sheep is also the agency charged with its protection and observation. Throughout the year, DFG rangers construct watering holes in remote places for the large animals and carefully monitor their behavior, migration routes and numbers.

*Rarely sighted
sentinels of the
desert.*

Tortoises

Warm spring weather brings hibernating tortoises out of their winter burrows, just in time to munch on wildflowers in bloom. These slow-moving, prehistoric-looking creatures have long been a favorite animal of little kids and their parents as well. Prime springtime viewing areas of desert tortoises includes Ivanpah and Fenner Valleys. Kelbaker Road, from Baker to Kelso, is another good place to see them; during the spring months, drive this road with special care for the safety of the tortoises.

If you spot one of these creatures, do not disturb it. Sit quietly and observe it, photograph it, record notes about it, but don't touch it, pick it up or bother it in any way.

The California Desert Tortoise is the state official reptile, fully protected by state and federal laws. Unfortunately, the tortoise's habitat—and population—have shrunk alarmingly in recent years.

In July of 1989, the U.S. Fish and Wildlife Service, in a rare emergency move, designated the desert tortoise as an endangered species. Citing evidence that the population of the reptile has declined up to sixty percent in some areas of the California desert, the agency agreed with several environmental groups working to protect the desert tortoise.

Human activities are largely the cause for the demise of the desert tortoise. Offroad vehicles are a major factor; not only do they occasionally run over the animals, but they crush their burrows and compact the earth.

Some unconscionable individuals have actually used the slow-moving tortoises for target practice—hardly a sporting or defensible undertaking.

The increasing raven population has also been blamed for the decline of the tortoise. The clever birds prey on tortoises and easily pick off the near-defenseless, lumbering creatures, especially the young. The problem has reached such levels that officials have considered shooting or poisoning the ravens to bring their numbers under control.

In recent years, the tortoise population has faced yet another threat—a respiratory virus that was once virtually unknown in the wild. They appear to have contracted the deadly virus from tortoises that were once kept as pets, then re-released into the wild. Today, the survival of these ancient animals, which have been called "living fossils," is in the hands of man.

Burros

Scores of burros were first brought to the desert a century ago by prospectors who loaded them up with supplies and headed west. The animals proved to be remarkably well-adapted to the climate and terrain; the descendants of those Gold Rush pack animals now number into several thousand wild animals who forage throughout the American desert.

Although we might enjoy a warm, fuzzy image of the wild burro, the truth is that it causes considerable damage to the environment.

The East Mojave provides these feral animals with many tasty treats. They destroy ground cover that protects many animals from predators and intense sunlight, and they trample the ground—and any unfortunate little animals that may get in their way.

Because they cause so much damage, no one seems to like the desert burro. Officials face several dilemmas in dealing with the animals; they are protected from inhumane treatment, but their populations are mandated to be controlled. The BLM currently manages an "Adopt-a-Burro" program, where individuals can adopt an animal at a very low price.

You may glimpse one of these skittish animals, but you probably won't get too close—and you shouldn't. These wild creatures have nasty temperaments and a swift kick.

Lizards

Many species of lizards live in the East Mojave. Dune dwelling fringe-toed lizards are a strange sight as they scoot over the sand on their hind legs, then dive into a dune and "swim" below the sand. The two-foot long Gila monster is well known but infrequently observed; its range is a few mountain ranges in the East Mojave.

Second in size only to the Gila monster, the chuckwalla is found on many a rocky slope. Sauromalu obsis ("fat bad lizard" by its Latin name) looks clumsy but it can scale a creosote bush and shake down the blossoms, which it eats. When frightened, the chuckwalla can puff out its loose skin and become immovably wedged in a rocky crevice.

Researchers say the large dominant males, called tyrants, gather harems and fiercely fend off rivals. Mating behavior among the chuckwalla has been described as erotic: females arouse males by rubbing and licking them.

CHAPTER NINE

East Mojave History

THE EAST MOJAVE DESERT has long been both a home and a gateway to the Far West. During the last century, however, it has also been viewed as a place that offers enough natural resources to support a specialized way of life. More recently, the view of the desert has been enlarged to one of a playground where cramped city dwellers can pursue recreational activities in wide open spaces. Accompanying and influencing these changing perceptions of man's relationship with the desert has been a growing controversy over which governmental agencies can best supervise, preserve and protect this land, and the activities it supports.

Earliest Habitation

During the Pleistocene Epoch, less than a half-million years ago, much of the area now known as the East Mojave was filled with the waters of Lake Manix, which supported not only abundant wildlife and vegetation, but a a significant human habitation as well.

Archeologists disagree about the time of human habitation; one school of thought refers to "early arrivals," the other to "late arrivals." Much of the controversy stems from the work of Dr. Louis S.B. Leakey, who supervised the massive excavation now called the Calico Early Man Site. The work, which began in 1964, was funded by the National Geographic Society. More than 11,000 artifacts have been found here in the alluvial material from the shores of ancient Lake Manix. Leakey determined them to be 200,000 years old. His belief seems to be supported by sophisticated uranium-thorium dating techniques and geomorphic testing of the soils that were conducted in 1980. Other experts believe that the earliest people first inhabited this area no more than 20,000 years ago.

Ancient rocks tell the story of the East Mojave's earliest inhabitants.

Indians practiced irrigation along the Colorado River.

Although no human remains of Early Man have been recovered from the Calico site, the chipped stone tools found appear to be evidence of the oldest human habitation in the Americas. To the average visitor to the site, however, whether the first habitation occurred 20,000 or 200,000 years ago hardly matters; the fact is, human beings have lived here a very long time, a period unimaginable to most of us.

Ancient Indians, who lived here up to 11,000 years ago, have left flaked and fluted stone artifacts and throwing sticks. Evidence of more recent dwellers, dated 11,000 to about 200 years ago, can be seen in other cultural artifacts including arrow points, mortars and pestles, pottery, petroglyphs and cave dwellings. Shells found in caves indicate that desert dwellers were engaged in trade with coastal Indians; evidence of turquoise mining near Clark Mountain and pottery shards found throughout the East Mojave lead archeologists and anthropologists to surmise that Pueblo Indians from the north and east regularly visited this area to mine and trade. The routes followed by these travelers later became major transportation routes through the desert.

Even as the area's weather changed and became more arid, and the water supply largely dried up, the Mojave River continued to flow year-round in many areas of the East Mojave. This availability of water ensured that humans could continue to inhabit the area.

The native people of the East Mojave—Piutes, Mojave and Chemehuevi—were well-adapted to their environment and managed to flourish in what we today consider a most inhospitable environment. They ate what was available: mesquite, prickly pear, tule roots and roasted agave blooms. They trapped and hunted deer and bighorn sheep, rodents, snakes, and birds in the New York and Providence Mountains. They used natural materials to craft what they needed—baskets from roots and willows, metates and mortars from stones for food preparation, needles and drills out of bones. They sought shelter where they found it; the Chemehuevi used the caves in the Providence Mountains—among them the present-day Mitchell Caverns—for more than 500 years.

Chemehuevi Indians, native people of the California Desert.

Although one would suppose that these nomadic hunter-gatherers had little leisure time, anthropologists believe that they did enjoy a rich oral tradition of story-telling and participated in many games. They engaged in ceremonial activities, often tied to the change of seasons, and decorated many areas of the East Mojave with petroglyphs— the meaning of which is still unclear. These artifacts can still be seen throughout the area; silent indicators of cultures very different from our own.

Spanish Exploration

Travel through the desert, although it posed many hardships and challenges to early explorers, was preferable to traveling through the mountains that served as a more formidable barrier to westward movement.

On his journey to the Coast from what is now known as the Gila Valley in Arizona, Spanish Explorer/Franciscan priest, Father Francisco Garcés began his travel through the East Mojave in 1776. Accompanied by three Mohave Indians, Fr. Garcés followed the Old Mojave Trail, from Piute Springs through the New York Mountains, over the Providence Mountains, Kelso Dunes and Soda Lake. He named the alkaline lake *"Arroyo de los Martires"* (River of the Martyrs). He also journeyed through Afton Canyon, which he called *"Sierra Pinta"* for the streaks of minerals that colored the canyon.

The natives not only led the friar along the route, but provided him with supplies and gifts. He described them as ". . . very quiet and inoffensive, and they hear with attention that which is told them of God."

The founding of the missions in California led to increased travel across the desert, and the establishment of the Spanish Trail—part of which became known as the Mojave Road—as the favored route west.

Father Francesco Garces passed through the Mojave in 1776. He was killed five years later by the Yumas.

Americans Push West

In 1826, Jedediah Strong Smith, one of the new breed of adventurous American fur trappers, followed the Colorado River from the north, then across the Mojave, along Garces' route. Other notable explorers who traveled through the Mojave include Kit Carson and John C. Frémont.

Frémont, who followed the Old Mojave Road in the 1840s, called it "the roughest and rockiest road we had ever seen." He continued, "Travellers through countries affording water and timber can have no conception of our intolerable thirst while journeying over the hot yellow sands of this elevated country, where the heated air seems to be entirely deprived of moisture."

Kit Carson

During the days when Manifest Destiny was the operating philosophy, America's western wilderness was seen as something to be conquered, settled and tamed. Forests were leveled, prairies were planted and the land was seen as virgin territory awaiting the hand of man.

The open space and barrenness of the desert was viewed by overland travelers as an obstacle to life itself; they hardly considered settling in such an environment. All they wanted to do was get through it as quickly and safely as possible. Fearing not only the harsh, unfamiliar land, but the Indians who lived there, travel through the desert was considered one of the most trying ordeals of the entire journey.

Westward expansion by Americans forced native people to change their customs, culture and way of dress.

Although the native population eyed the intruders on their land as warily as the pioneers regarded them, their numbers soon declined, and their land was gradually lost as the newcomers settled in. As was the case throughout the West, cowboy-and-Indian stories were more than the stuff of legend; there were many fierce clashes between the Indians and white travelers in the East Mojave.

To wagon trains
heading west, the
Mojave was often
the worst obstacle.

The isolated
ruins of Fort
Piute.

Military Then and Now

Because wagon trains and stage coaches were frequently attacked along the Old Mojave Road, the United States government established a number of army outposts. Fort Piute, Camp Rock Springs and Camp Cady were built in the 1860s to house the soldiers and escorts assigned to accompany and protect immigrants and mail carriers. These tiny camps, situated in such lonely territory, were never staffed by more than a few soldiers at a time; desertion and understaffing were always problems at the Mojave desert forts.

By the late 1860s, the Indian populations were decimated by war, disease and displacement to reservations. With their superior firepower, technology and the power of law on their side, the newcomers simply overcame the resistance of the native people and claimed control of the land. As the Indians were subdued, the need for military outposts was lessened, and all of them were abandoned in just a decade. They stand in ruins to this day.

But the open land of the desert has continued to appeal to military planners. In the 1940s, General George S. Patton trained World War II troops in war games conducted throughout the California Desert; evidence of the Iron Mountain Camp (located near Joshua Tree National Monument)—tank tracks and other scars on the land—remain distinct nearly a half-century later. In the early 1960s, Operation Desert Strike was conducted in the East Mojave. One hundred thousand men, and a massive amount of equipment, spent a month training near Fort Piute. A marker on U.S. 95 pays tribute to the operation.

The coming of the railroad displaced native people in the California desert and all over the west.

Calling the 1964 war games an example of "very grave destruction," Edmund C. Jaeger

observed, "It appears that little if any thought was given to the preservation of the natural amenities of this magnificent sweep of fragile desert. Not in a hundred years can the damage be repaired by nature even if no further exercises take place."

His comments characterize the prevailing position in opposition to the military's use of the desert. While the branches of the military continue to view the desert as a vast expanse of open land, especially well-suited to their training exercises, others see it as a unique and fragile ecosystem that may be forever damaged by high-impact activities.

The military's use of the desert is not limited to the land itself. The airspace above the East Mojave is considered prime for testing and training flights for exotic supersonic jets. Unsuspecting drivers or hikers are frequently surprised when they hear the sound of fast-moving military jets swooping low overhead.

Camp Ibis, located in the East Mojave, was the site of military maneuvers, as were many other sites in the California. Desert.

Tank in a live fire war-game

Mining

Gold Rush fever of the 1800s prompted men to look at the land not only for the crops it might support, but for what riches lay beneath the soil. Since the desert was so obviously lacking in resources to support life, it stood to reason to many that it must be hiding much good deep below. Turn-of-the-century author and California booster George Wharton James expressed the prevailing sentiment of his time when he wrote: "A place which is obviously so cursed that nothing will grow on it must have been created by the Lord of all things for some purpose and the only purpose it could possibly have was to carry minerals hidden somewhere below its forbidden surface."

Because the East Mojave has such a varied geology you might expect a wide variety of mineral resources—and truly an impressive array of minerals has been discovered. Gold, silver, zinc, iron ore and copper are among the more common metallic elements that have been successfully mined. Discoveries of these elements led to the establishment of many mining camp towns in the East Mojave. Despite the harshness of the land and the extreme climate, the towns of Ivanpah, Hart and Vanderbilt sprang up to serve the needs of the miners. In the pages of this guide, and during your travels through the East Mojave, you'll learn more about these one-time boom towns.

During the 1940s, Kaiser Steel Company established the Vulcan Iron Ore Mine in the Providence Mountains. The successful mine created a short-lived boom in the town of Kelso, where most of the miners lived with their families. By the end of the decade, the mine shut down, and the population of Kelso declined from a high of 1,500 down to just a few hundred.

Abandoned mining sites honeycomb many of the mountains throughout the East Mojave and can still be found by hikers and explorers. (Use great care around such sites; it's not safe to enter them.)

Over the years, as human use of the East Mojave has changed, so too has the prevailing land ethic. What was once seen as digging and scratching at the earth now looks like the scarring and misuse of a fragile land. Today, while there are several responsible mining operations unearthing necessary minerals for the public good, there are also far too many shoddy operations—many based on bogus claims—that are simply ecologically as well as

One mode of hauling borax—more powerful than a 20-mule team, circa 1887.

Francis M. "Borax" Smith, borax mining magnate.

economically indefensible. These latter claims, conservationists say, must go.

Central to the mining issue is the century old General Mining Law of 1872, which allows individuals to stake a claim on the land after a valuable mineral deposit has been discovered. These claims are purchased for little money and require few improvements on the land in order to maintain them or a small fee. Claims can be purchased, willed or inherited. Although the federal government is required to put each claim to a "prudent man and marketability test," many questionable mining claims go unchallenged year after year.

Railroads are not just a nostalgic reminder of days gone by; many lines are still in service.

The image of the grizzled old miner staking his claim, and scratching out a living on the earth is romantic and quite appealing. But mining in the desert is no longer done by a lone individual armed with a pick-axe and shovel. It's conducted by major mining corporations which use sophisticated methods to extract minerals from the ground.

The Mountain Pass area, near Clark Mountain, contains a rich mine of the rare earth element bastnasite, along with other rare earths with the science fiction sounding names of cerium, lanthanum and neodymium. These rare earth minerals are used in research related to the high-tech field of superconductivity, along with petroleum-processing, metallurgical and glass-making applications.

A proposal to allow cyanide heap leaching for gold at Castle Mountain is a corporate mining project that was bitterly opposed by environmentalists until an agreement was finally reached.

From hard rock miner to "mayor" of Nipton: Jerry Freeman welcomes guests to the town he purchased in 1984.

Ranching

"What are they doing out here?" visitors ask when they see forlorn cows standing in the meager shade of a Joshua tree.

Many a dirt road drive through the East Mojave results in an encounter with range cattle. Although the East Mojave is a land of sparse vegetation, cattle ranching has long been considered a way of life here.

The animals were probably first brought here by the military, which maintained small herds for food. When the military pulled out, the cattle were left behind. The turn-of-the-century Rock Springs Land and Cattle Company, which at one time maintained a herd of nearly 5,000 cattle, was the most successful ranching operation in the East Mojave; today the OX Cattle Company is the leading operation. Fewer than two dozen individuals ranch here today; it's become an unprofitable and difficult way of life.

"What are cows doing out here?" visitors wonder.

Railroad

Although it was intended to run from Nevada to the Pacific, the closest the T & T got to a water source was Broad Dry Lake.

The coming of the railroad to the desert linked the East Mojave to the rest of the world, making settlement attractive, and business more profitable.

The mostly small, private railroad lines were established by wealthy industrialists who envisioned increasing their fortunes by transporting desert riches to major shipping points. Francis Marion "Borax" Smith constructed the Tidewater and Tonopah line to service his borax mine in the Death Valley area.

The Nevada Southern Railroad, operated from the 1893 until 1923. It served the tiny towns of Goffs and Lanfair, Barnwell and Vontrigger. Homesteaders, ranchers and miners who settled in the area were able to ship their supplies, cattle and ores on the line. The railroad declined due to a combination of factors: damage to the lines from shifting sands, flash flooding and disuse as the area's population dwindled.

The Union Pacific, which came to the East Mojave during World War I, runs trains through the East Mojave; freight lines rumble through regularly, and a single passenger train runs from Los Angeles to Las Vegas daily. Taking the train through the desert allows passengers to view parts of the East Mojave inaccessible by motor vehicle. And no one can deny the romance of the rails. As the song goes, "There's something about a train."

Recreation

The desert provides open spaces, solitude and quiet—all of which are in short supply in congested urban areas. City dwellers looking for adventure have found it in various forms in the desert—some which have virtually no impact on the environment, others which have alarmingly destructive consequences.

Hiking, photography, painting, bird-watching, astronomy, and other low-impact activities allow desert visitors to enjoy the environment while preserving its integrity for years to come. The same cannot be said, however, for those who engage in activities such as riding off-road vehicles irresponsibly, shooting and committing acts of vandalism.

Particularly offensive to many visitors are off-highway vehicles—dune buggies, motorcycles and all-terrain vehicles—which have come under fire by conservationists for their destructive effects on the land, air quality, and peacefulness of the environment.

Many of the prime spots in the East Mojave are accessible only by dirt road; there's no question that four-wheel drive vehicles are well-suited to desert travel. Those who responsibly tour into the heart of the desert on dirt roads (including the historic Mojave Road and Heritage Trail) may be delighted with the richness of the experience.

But far too many "free playing" off-highway vehicle users have not acted responsibly. While off-road riding in the desert is strictly prohibited by law, many choose to ignore the rules, and tear up land in the process. Off-highway vehicles scar the fragile desert land, and cause extensive damage to plants and animals that inhabit it.

The East Mojave offers some of the most peaceful and secluded camping in California.

CHAPTER TEN

Managing the Mojave

WHEN THE EAST MOJAVE National Scenic Area was established in 1980 it was placed under the administration of the Bureau of Land Management, part of the U.S. Department of the Interior.

The BLM was assigned the task of protecting the scenic, cultural and recreational features of 1.5 acres of desert, while also overseeing mining, ranching and off-highway vehicle use.

The U.S. Bureau of Land Management came into being in 1946 when the General Land Office (often referred to as "the government's real estate agent") and the U.S. Grazing Service were combined into a single agency. During the Bureau's early years, desert administrators and their counterparts throughout the West operated under confusing and sometimes conflicting federal mandates.

Passage of the Federal Land Policy Management Act (FLPMA) of 1976 helped nudge the BLM into more modern ways of managing its vast holdings of government land. "Flipma," as it's usually referred to, provided, among other things, that: (1) Outdoor recreation be a principal or major use of public lands; (2) BLM evaluate all public lands for their wilderness values and make recommendations to Congress of Wilderness Area designation; (3) BLM manage established wilderness areas under the provisions of the Wilderness Act of 1964; (4) BLM be empowered to have a program of law enforcement and a ranger force to patrol its most environmentally sensitive properties. (BLM's very first rangers were assigned to the California desert.)

Long before the federal government enacted its many Acts and Plans, the East Mojave Desert was known to possess unusual combinations of plants and animals, striking geology and scenery,

BLM's emblem introduced in 1953 illustrated the agency's development and industry orientation. Later logos emphasize the beauty of public lands.

115

and a great potential for recreation. However, it was not until the whole California desert began to be (re)evaluated by the federal government during the 1970s that the desert in general, and the Mojave in particular, began receiving the attention—and protection—it had long deserved.

The Bureau began operating its Scenic Area under the framework of its California Desert Conservation Area Plan. This plan, which cost $8 million, was formulated after a four-year study. The BLM gathered an astonishing 40,000 public responses for its plan, believed to be the largest regional planning effort ever attempted in the U.S.

BLM's Desert Plan was gigantic in scope, as was the land it covered—25 million acres of California desert. In 1988, the Bureau began managing the East Mojave under a more specific plan—the East Mojave National Scenic Area Management Plan.

When BLM's long-awaited Desert Plan was completed, a *Los Angeles Times* editorial, perhaps summing up the mood of many citizens who contributed to the grueling planning process, stated: "The plan appears to protect the interests of preservationists while recognizing the needs of miners, ranchers and utility companies. It is a balanced plan no group will be entirely happy with and that's a good sign."

Particularly unhappy with the plan and BLM's interpretation of its mandate were environmentalists who claimed that the agency, wedded by law to its multiple use doctrine, had over-emphasized commodity production and utilitarian use over wilderness preservation and wildlife management. Critics claimed that Congress gave BLM an impossible task—a balancing act impossible to perform.

To the agency's critics, the most glaring example of mismanagement of fragile desert resources was its supervision of off-highway vehicle use. The Barstow to Las Vegas motorcycle races through the East Mojave were particularly upsetting to conservationists.

At issue is the preservation of the desert's unspoiled, wide-open spaces.

Until halted in 1989, the B-V race was an extremely emotional issue for both sides. (Unfortunately for the public's awareness of the desert, race day seemed to be the only day that the major media ventured anywhere near the East Mojave.)

The desert debate, which had focused on mining, OHV use and the quantity of land that the BLM had proposed in its plans to set aside as wilderness, heated up sharply in 1987 when California Senator Alan Cranston introduced his California Desert Protection Act to Congress. The far-reaching bill attempted to create three new national parks: two were "upgrades" of Joshua Tree and Death Valley national monuments, while the third proposed a Mojave National Park. The latter park was to be formed largely from land included within the bounds of BLM's East Mojave National Scenic Area.

Senator Cranston and many in the environmental community, including the Sierra Club and the California Desert Protection League, believed that only National Park Service management could adequately protect these desert lands. "The biggest reason [for Mojave National Park]," stated Cranston, "is that the desert is being scarred forever, its natural state destroyed by off-road vehicles that are not controlled adequately as to where they can go, and by those who seek development."

Other conservationists at the time figured that the East Mojave could be managed in a more park-like manner without actually stripping the BLM of the East Mojave and transferring it to the National Park Service. They contended that the BLM was financially hamstrung from implementing its desert

Restrictions on off-road vehicles are a hotly debated issue in the desert.

Signs of times past: Graphic opposition to Senator Cranston's bills.

plans; with more money and more manpower, the agency would be a more vigilant guardian of the Mojave.

The BLM itself claimed that it had shed much of its commodity development orientation and was a true resource management agency. Many BLM rangers and administrators insisted that their agency gave the East Mojave top priority; the National Park Service would adjudge Mojave National Park a very low priority, they argued.

After the California Desert Bill was first introduced in 1987, it was modified and reintroduced again and again over the years. Rep. Mel Levine introduced similar legislation in the U.S. House of Representatives.

To say that legislation proposing Mojave National Park created a lot of controversy in these parts is like saying the desert has a lot of sand. Both sides produced mountains of literature and hours of videotape supporting their positions on everything from the effects of off-highway vehicle noise on the kangaroo rat's hearing to the use of cyanide in gold mining.

To mention but five of the many hotly contested issues brought up during discussion of the various desert park bills:

Wilderness—How primitive, how unaffected by man's works must a landscape be in order to be classified as a wilderness? Will wilderness areas in the East Mojave Desert lock-out most human endeavors or simply encourage a more gentle use of the land?

Mining—How much and what kinds should be allowed? Can antiquated mining laws be updated? To what extent should individuals and corporations be held responsible for restoring land they damage?

Ranching—Is this arid land anyplace to raise a cow? What are the effects of grazing? Overgrazing?

Off-Highway Vehicles—How many thousands of miles of dirt road are enough? Is the surface of the desert as fragile as environmentalists contend, or as resilient as off-roaders claim?

Wildlife—How severely have tortoises, bighorn sheep and other desert dwellers been affected by damage to their habitat?

Over the years the debate assumed several dimensions—economic, aesthetic, moral, political, even philosophical. Elden Hughes, Chairman of the California Desert Protection League, repeatedly stated that the desert was more than an issue to him—it was a passion. This self-proclaimed desert rat spent—and still spends—most of his spare time in the desert photographing everything from grand landscapes to rare flowers, and exploring places virtually unknown to even those familiar with the East Mojave. "I've traveled this desert all my life,"

How much of this land shall be set aside as wilderness? an important question in the desert debate.

he stated. "It's park quality, and the Park Service is best able to protect it."

Soon after taking office, California Senator Dianne Feinstein introduced the California Desert Protection Act of 1993. Like the Senator Cranston-sponsored bills before it, the legislation was designed to create national parks of Death Valley and Joshua Tree national monuments, as well as establish a new Mojave National Park. The bill called for a nearly 1.5-acre park, with about half that acreage set aside in wilderness areas. Upon passage of the legislation, the Secretary of the Interior must prepare a management plan for the new park within three years.

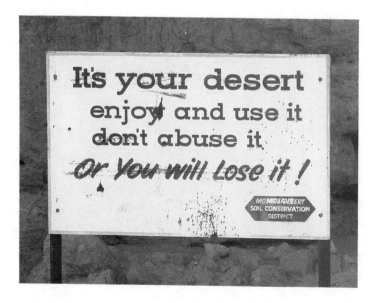

"I confess that the fascination of the untamed desert has proved to be of too subtle a quality for words of mine to render. That would necessarily be true, of course, of anybody's attempt in any field of Nature: but it would be tenfold true with respect to the desert."

—Joseph Smeaton Chase

PART III

On Tour: Travels Through the East Mojave

Botanic diversity in the Providence Mountains.

CHAPTER ELEVEN

Providence Mountains Area And Beyond

ONE OF THE MOST DIVERSE and certainly most accessible destinations in the East Mojave, the Providence Mountains area, is an excellent first stop for desert explorations. With dramatic mile-high peaks as a backdrop, this area features a variety of plant communities, an easy canyon hike, a nature trail and nearby campground, and ranger-led tours of one of the most interesting limestone caves in the West.

Located off Essex Road, 17 miles north of Interstate 40, this area is a must-see for East Mojave visitors. As you travel north on Essex Road, you'll see the massive Providence Mountains looming to the northwest. The highest peaks in the range are 6,996-foot Fountain Peak and 7,171-foot Edgar Peak, both located just west of the Providence Mountains State Recreation Area visitor center.

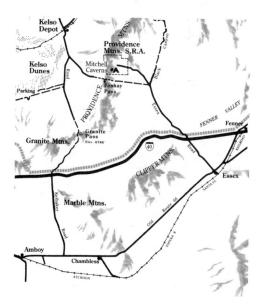

The Providence Mountains

The Providence Mountains, limestone peaks intermixed with ancient volcanic, sedimentary and crystalline formations, are among the tallest mountains in the East Mojave. They rise above the Clipper Valley and Kelso Basin; the west end forms a 600-foot escarpment—one of the most prominent views in this land of basin and range faulting.

During the 1880s, the Bonanza King Mine was a major source of silver in the area. The town of Providence was founded by the miners; its population hovered around 500 until the mine operations ceased in 1887. More than 60 million dollars worth of silver was mined from Bonanza King. The ruins of the old mine and the ghost town of Providence can be seen today, but it takes a strenuous rock-climbing adventure to get to them.

These mineral-rich mountains were also the site of a more recent major mining project. During World War II, when demand for iron ore was at an all-time high, the Vulcan Mine, located near Foshay Pass, was operated by Kaiser Steel. More than two million tons of ore were mined here; the mining activity caused a boom in the nearby town of Kelso. But the mine was shut down in 1947, turning Kelso into a virtual ghost town once again.

The Providence Mountains State Recreation Area is an island of state-owned land within the East Mojave Desert. In 1954, the state purchased the land from Ida Mitchell, the widow of Jack Mitchell who developed the area and the caverns that bear his name. Be sure to visit the area's main attraction, Mitchell Caverns, as well as the visitor center and Mary Beal Nature Trail. Campers can stay at the small campground, walkers may wish to take the hike up Crystal Springs Canyon.

The views in this area are spectacular; from the Overlook Trail near the campground (elevation 4,300 feet) you can see mountains and mesas, valleys and sand dunes. The view of Clipper Valley to the east stretches a hundred open miles. To put that distance in perspective, consider that the entire Los Angeles Basin would fit into the empty valley below.

Mitchell Caverns

Jack and Ida Mitchell struck it rich in real estate in Los Angeles in the 1920s. Speculating that there might be a tourism boom in the desert, they staked a claim in the Providence Mountains after

learning of the magnificent caverns located in the range. When they lost most of their fortune during the early 1930s, the Mitchells loaded up their Model-T and moved to the desert.

The hard-working couple lived in the caves for nearly a year while they constructed stone accommodations for overnight visitors, built a road and a trail to the caves, staircases and other amenities, still hoping to attract tourists to the limestone caverns. The hogan-style home they built for themselves is embedded with bits of glass, rocks, gemstones and petrified wood. Their patience and perseverance paid off, and the visitors began to arrive. The Mitchells led their guests on candle-lit tours of the caverns.

Stalactites and stalagmites, flowstone, cave spaghetti, cave shields and cave ribbons are among the formations seen in the cool caverns that maintain a constant temperature of 65 degrees year-round. From September through June, you can join a ranger-led tour of the two main chambers, but it's not quite as romantic as it was in the early years. Stairs, railings and electric lights have

Some people smile in the evening;
Some of them smile in the morn,
But the guy worth while
Is the guy who can smile
When his teeth are all gone

Sincerely Yours,
Jack Mitchell.

been installed, and rangers carry flashlights and point out particularly interesting formations. They're an enthusiastic, informative lot, and the tour is likely to be quite memorable. Serious spelunkers can make special arrangements for entrance to Winding Stair Cave.

The Mitchells named the two chambers, the first called "El Pakiva," (the Devil's House); the second, "Tecopa," (for a Chemehuevi chieftain). The Indian names are a tribute to the Chemehuevi people, who lived in the caves for nearly 500 years. Anthropologists and archeologists have recovered pottery shards, arrowheads and food caches; they conclude that native people used these caverns, probably on a seasonal basis, for shelter, storage and even certain ceremonies. Young boys were probably left in the darkness of the caves as part of a coming-of-age ritual.

Stalactites and stalagmites, flowstone and cave shields— hardly what travelers expect to find in arid desert lands.

Imagine the life of the Chemeheuvis when they stayed in these caves and mountains. While the men hunted for game, the women tended the children, wove baskets and sandals and prepared food. When the men returned from the hunt, often loaded with quail, deer and rabbits, they were enthusiastically welcomed by the rest of the community. After a successful hunt, they celebrated with ritual games and ceremonies; music was an important part of their social activities. Close your eyes a moment and see if you can't conjure up the thin, haunting tones of a four-hole cane flute, the chant of a shaman, the vocal response of the assembled community. These mountains and quiet caverns once reverberated with sound.

The caves were created over several million years. The limestone rock was once the bottom of an ancient ocean; geologic forces uplifted and tilted it high above the body of water. The pressures formed cracks and crevices in the limestone, the very beginning of the cave formation. About 12 million years ago, the earth above the limestone was covered with a thick rain forest. As the saturating rains fell, the rainwater absorbed carbon dioxide from the decomposing plant matter. The slightly acidic water seeped into the cracks and crevices in the limestone and expanded them into caves filled with water.

As the weather changed and became drier over the next several thousand years, the groundwater level lowered, the water-filled caves emptied. When rainfall once again increased, the acidic water seeped into the caves and began depositing a tiny spot of calcite with every drop. Over many thousands of years, the calcite grew into the grand stalactites, stalagmites and other cave formations that can be seen here today.

At present, the caves are not growing; experts speculate that they will eventually—thousands of years from now—weather away and disappear.

Ranger John Kelso-Shelton explains the wonders of Mitchell Caverns.

Mary Beal Nature Study Trail

The self-guiding nature trail near the visitor center is an excellent introduction to desert plants and animals. Pick up a booklet at the visitor center and take a walk through the garden that includes hedgehog, barrel, prickly pear and pancake cactus, as well as yucca, creosote, cat's claw and cholla.

The trail honors Mary Beal, who, at the turn of the century, was sent to the desert by her physician. Her health drastically improved in the dry climate, and she spent a half-century exploring the Providence Mountains and other high-desert locales. The former librarian discovered and classified hundreds of desert plants and wildflowers. The trail was dedicated in 1952.

Naturalist Mary Beal regained her health and recorded a wealth of botanical information when she moved to the East Mojave.

Crystal Springs Canyon Trail

The one-mile-long Crystal Springs Canyon Trail leads into the pinyon pine- and juniper-dotted Providence Mountains by way of Crystal Canyon. Bighorn sheep often travel through this canyon, but it's more likely that you'll spot a cottontail rabbit, antelope ground squirrel, or one of the many species of birds that inhabit the area.

CHAPTER TWELVE

Kelso

SITUATED IN THE HEART of the East Mojave Desert are two scenic wonders: Kelso Depot and Kelso Dunes. One man-made, one natural, both stand as reminders of the inevitability of change over time. Easily accessible from good roads, they are among the most frequently visited sites in the desert.

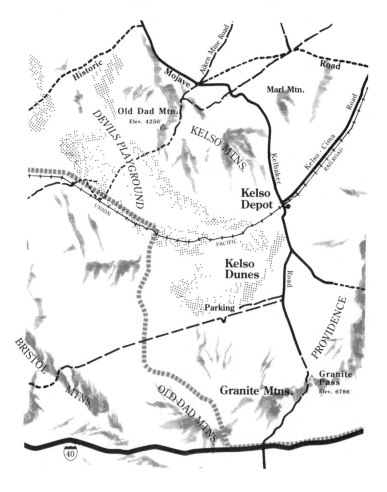

Kelso Depot

Kelso station today.

In 1906, the completion of the railroad between Salt Lake City and the port facilities in Los Angeles led to the modest development of the tiny town of Kelso. As the only railway between the two major cities, it grew in importance with the emergence of Los Angeles as a major urban area. Because Kelso was one of the few places in the desert with access to dependable water sources, it was considered a good location for a railroad stopping point.

Steam locomotives, still in wide use at the time, took on boiler water in Kelso before they chugged up the long Cima grade—a climb of 2,000 feet in eighteen miles. Later, railroad officials realized Kelso was a good location for a stopover point for railroad crews to rest and obtain supplies.

The Spanish style depot was built by Union Pacific in 1924. This distinctive 50- by 150-foot, two-story wooden structure was designed with a red-tiled roof, graceful arches, and a red brick platform. It featured several small rooms which provided overnight accommodations for railroad employees, a telegraph office, and a waiting room for passengers. Over the years, a restaurant area was established in the depot. Nicknamed "The Beanery," the restaurant occasionally served meals to the public, and several large rooms located in the basement of the facility served as a community center for local residents.

During the war years, the population of Kelso increased to nearly 2,000 residents—primarily railroad employees and workers at the Vulcan Iron Ore Mine located in the nearby Providence Mountains. The railroad was used extensively to haul the mined ore to its milling site in Fontana. But when the mine shut down in 1947, the town's population dwindled. Rail services also declined.

The depot continued to be open through the mid-1980s, although it ceased to be a railroad stop for passengers after World War II. Visitors picnicked on the oasis-like lawn, ate at the restaurant and generally enjoyed the Mediterranean ambience of the charming buiding. When Union Pacific officials decided to demolish the historic building in 1985, local citizens, governmental officials, environmentalists and a host of others formed a coalition to fight the plan.

The group, known as the Kelso Depot Fund, was successful in its efforts to save the depot, and it continues to work for its preservation and restoration. The building will be used as a visitor information center for the East Mojave. Other more speculative plans include re-opening a restaurant, a conference center or a railroad museum.

The availability of water at Kelso makes it an important stop for migratory birds; the manicured lawn and cottonwood trees provide an oasis-like feeling. And the historic architecture lends a stately elegance to the once-again tiny town with a population of only two dozen. Although they no longer stop here, freight cars and passenger trains regularly rumble through Kelso, adding a nostalgic touch to this picturesque setting.

The one-room schoolhouse at Kelso also served as home for the teacher. Circa 1908.

Kelso Dunes

One of the more spectacular sights in the East Mojave is Kelso Dunes. This 45-square-mile formation of magnificently sculpted sand dunes is the most extensive dune field in the West. Some dunes tower over 700 feet high.

The dunes are actually built up from the particulate remains of mountains worn away long ago. Prevailing winds create the dunes as they blow sand particles from the Mojave River Sink, across the Devil's Playground. Blocked from further movement by the Providence Mountains to the east, the individual grains are then deposited at the dune site.

The tips of desert grasses on the dunes scribe 360° arcs with the whirling winds.

Kelso Dunes are referred to as "booming dunes" for the low vibrational sounds that are created when the sand made of polished grains of rose quartz slides over the underlying surface. The low rumbling sounds emitted by "booming dunes" have been compared to the sound of a chorus or a mythological siren. Everywhere they occur, from Egypt to Libya to the Kelso Dunes of California, they have become the stuff of folklore and legend.

An old story tells of a teamster who started off across the dunes with a wagonload of whiskey to replenish the supplies of the saloons in Kelso. A violent sandstorm arose, and forced the wagonmaster to unhitch his team to wait out the storm. But when he returned to reclaim his property with its important contents, he could not locate it. Legend has it that the sounds that can be heard coming from the dunes on cold, clear nights are really the celebrations of the ghosts of the old teamster and his friends, who have finally located their precious load and are reveling in their discovery.

Since the Kelso Dunes have been closed to off-road vehicles since 1973, they've been relatively protected from the kind of damage that has reduced some of California's dune formations to barren piles of sand.

More than 100 varieties of plants live on or near the dunes, including sand verbenas, desert primrose and native grasses. Mesquite and creosote grow on the lower dunes.

Dune-dwelling animals include several species of birds, rodents, sidewinders, lizards and kit foxes. Several insects are found here, and nowhere else in the world, such as the Kelso Dune Jerusalem Cricket.

The dunes are a reminder of nature's power and the never-ending process of change over eons. Photographers and artists attempt to capture the stunning qualities of these dunes, but nothing compares to a first-hand visit.

Prime times to visit the dunes are at daybreak and at sundown. The early morning rays cast a rose-colored glow on the sand, and the fading late afternoon sun gives a bluish-purple appearance. The hike takes at least three hours; plan your trek so you're not out on the dunes during the midday heat. Always bring water and a snack.

The Kelso dunes may boom, but they still offer hikers plenty of opportunity for solitude and quiet times.

The Kelso Dunes provide a fine vantage point from which to gain a stunning view of the East Mojave. But to get to the top of the shifting sands requires some hard work. Although the hike is only three miles round trip, it is demanding, sometimes discouraging. There's a lot of one step forward, two steps back, especially as you near the top of the ridge. Take your time, and enjoy the experience; it's not every day you get to play in a giant sandbox.

After parking in the designated area, simply head north toward the dunes. Carefully pick your way cross-country. As you near the dunes you'll notice many native grasses growing on the sand; you may observe evidence of the circular winds that are prevalent in this area. Frequently the tips of tall grasses serve as a radius, scribing a circular pattern from their base as they're moved by the winds.

You may also observe the tracks of kangaroo rats, lizards and other small animals that scamper lightly across the surface of the sand. And you may wish you were a little lighter, especially on the last leg of the ascent of the dunes, when you may find yourself knee-deep in soft sand.

Take the time to rest when you get to the top, sit for awhile and contemplate the beauty of the desert surroundings. View the Kelso Mountains to the north, the Bristol Mountains to the southwest, the Granite Mountains to the south and the Providence Mountains to the east.

While the trek up the mountain of sand can be slow going, the quick trip down is guaranteed to make you feel like a carefree kid. As you scamper down the dunes with reckless abandon you'll create sand slides and mini-avalanches, and you may hear the characteristic booming sound of the Kelso Dunes as the sand slips across the underlying layer.

CHAPTER THIRTEEN

Hole-in-the-Wall

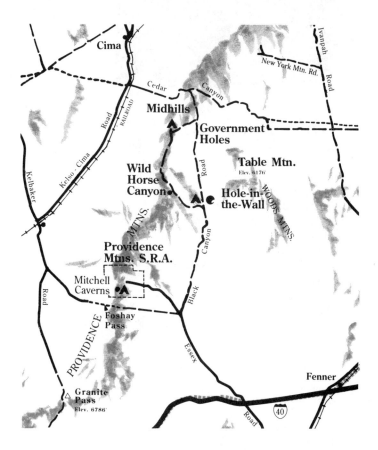

THE CENTRAL AREA of the East Mojave, highlighted by two popular camping areas at Hole-in-the-Wall and Mid Hills, is characterized by its high elevation, classic basin-and-range terrain—flattop peaks separated by dry valleys—unusual volcanic rock formations and outstanding views of the surrounding sandscape.

Tabletop mesas are common in this basin and range geology of the East Mojave.

The pinyon pine-juniper woodland flourishes in the high elevation of the central East Mojave. Visitors find it a welcome sight to view large trees in the middle of the desert. The trees provide shade, and the elevation ensures cooler temperatures than those found in the surrounding lower desert. It's one of the few places in the East Mojave where mid-summer camping can be considered; daytime temperatures usually reach only into the 90s. In the winter, however, snowstorms are common, while springtime usually brings colorful blooms. Snow flurries and hail, although unusual, may occur into mid-May.

Driving to the region on Black Canyon Road, you'll note the magnificent Providence Mountains to the west, and in the distance, the smaller Kelso and Marl Ranges. To the east are the steep Woods Mountains and one of the East Mojave's most distinctive landmarks, Table Mountain, a 6,176-foot mesa that juts up from the desert floor. It can be seen from many vantage points throughout the central East Mojave.

This is open country, reminiscent of the Old West, complete with barbed wire fences, sagebrush, range cattle, occasional windmills, and views that go on forever.

In 1989, Wildhorse Canyon Road, which loops from Hole-in-the-Wall Campground to Mid Hills Campground, was declared the nation's first official "Back Country Byway." Anyone who drives the eleven-mile, horseshoe-shaped road will agree that it's worthy of this honor.

Beginning at Hole-in-the-Wall, the Wildhorse Canyon Back Country Byway crosses wide-open country dotted with cholla and in season, delicate purple, yellow, white and red wildflowers. Dramatic volcanic slopes and flat-top mesas tower over this low desert. Proceeding northward, visitors will encounter a landscape of sagebrush, then an inviting pinyon-juniper woodland.

The road takes travelers from the 3,500-foot level at Hole-in-the-Wall to mile-high Mid Hills Campground. In fact, one of the attractions of the road is the diversity of scenery that changes with the elevation. If you're very lucky, you'll spot deer or even a bighorn sheep on the rocky slopes above the road.

Three of the most prominent East Mojave plants—cholla, yucca and Joshua tree.

Mid Hills Campground

Two miles west of Black Canyon Road, this campground is located in a pinyon pine-juniper woodland and offers outstanding views. This mile-high place, filled with sagebrush and piles of granite rock, resembles the Great Basin Desert of Nevada and Utah.

Mid Hills, so named because of its location midway between the Providence and New York Mountains, is a unique vantage point from which to observe the East Mojave's biggest and most distinctive ranges. To the north, can be seen the cafe au lait-colored Pinto Mountain, to the west lie the rolling Kelso Sand Dunes.

The isolated campground's central location offers two major features that appeal to those wanting to "get away from it all." It's easy to reach, yet it feels like it's miles from nowhere. With more than two dozen well-spaced campsites, it allows visitors a sense of privacy, while incorporating a feeling of campground community. At the north end of the campground, looking northwest, is the East Mojave's best view of Cima Dome, the 75-square-mile formation of uplifted once-molten rock.

Some desert rats say the hiking trail linking Mid Hills Campground with Hole-in-the-Wall, eight miles to the south, is the best in the East Mojave.

The eight-mile, mostly downhill route between Mid Hills and Hole-in-the-Wall is a memorable hike.

Desert rats have named this distinctive formation "Dromedary Rock." It's located approximately midway between Mid Hills and Hole-in-the-Wall.

The hike between Mid Hills and Hole-in-the-Wall is an adventurous excursion through a diverse desert environment. You'll see piles of rounded boulders at the northern end, basin and range table-top mesas at the southern end of the trail. Along the way, you'll encounter large pinyon trees, an array of colorful cactus and lichen-covered granite rocks. The views of Table Mountain, Wild Horse Mesa and the Providence Range are unparalled.

One of the most intriguing aspects of the Mid Hills area is the dominant plant life—the pinyon pine-juniper forest. During Pleistocene times, a few hundred thousand years ago, these cone-bearing trees flourished throughout the Mojave. As the weather became more and more arid, the range of these trees was restricted to higher elevations, which provided sufficient precipitation for their growth.

The tall, fragrant, two-needle pines that are so prominent in this area were once an important food source. In the fall, when the nuts were ripe and most plentiful, the Chemehuevi, Piute, and other native people, traveled to the places where the sturdy cone-bearing trees lived. They broke the pine cones off the trees, then roasted them to gather the nuts hidden inside.

Piute Pinenut Prayer

The pinenuts belong to the
mountain
We ask the mountain that we
may have of its pinenuts.
We would eat.

Pointing out a
few of the sights
in this classic
devil's garden in
Wildhorse
Canyon.

Today, hungry hikers enjoy collecting the creamy-white nuts; their tangy, vaguely piney taste make an interesting trailside snack. But be sure to take a few home; pinenuts (also known as pignolas) are delicious when added to a salad, or sprinkled atop pasta tossed with pesto sauce.

The small, twisted juniper tree is the other dominant plant of this area. This unique pine bears distinctive blue berries in the spring; they are the source from which gin is made.

Also thriving in this area is the low sagebrush scrub community, with its pungently fragrant sage, assorted cacti, and springtime wildflowers.

Hole-in-the-Wall

This is one of the most interesting and enjoyable locations in the desert. Hole-in-the-Wall provides visitors with a camping area, outstanding views of the surrounding mountains, and an unforgettable hiking experience.

Directly east of the campground are the Woods Mountains. The range features appropriately named Rustlers Canyon, an out-of-the way place where cattle rustlers and various outlaws once hid out from lawmen.

Although the location of the small campground at Hole-in-the-Wall (elevation 4,200 feet) is pleasant enough to attract campers, bird-watchers and others who just want to "stay-put," more adventurous types find the highlight of a trip to Hole-in-the-Wall is exploring the wondrous volcanic formations that form its backdrop. In the spring and fall, visit the Information Center located here.

Immediately west of the campground is a maze of volcanic rocks that descend first into Banshee Canyon, then into a large, open desert box canyon named Wildhorse Canyon. The two canyons couldn't be more dissimilar—they provide the visitor with a glimpse of the diversity of the East Mojave Desert.

Hikers once used ropes and ladders to descend into Banshee Canyon from the campground area; today the descent is accomplished by negotiating two sets of iron rings that have been set into the rock. Maneuvering through the rings is not particularly difficult for those who are reasonably agile and take their time. But acrophobes or claustrophobes may want to pass on this adventure.

Walter Ford, in a 1941 article published in "Desert" magazine, recounted his experiences in Hole-in-the-Wall: "With a 100-foot rope securely tied around a large boulder I crawled over the overhanging ledge and found myself dangling in mid-air with the next projecting rock 25 feet below!

*Co-author
explores
Hole-in-the-
Wall.*

We had assumed that there would be footholds all the way down but here was a condition with which we had not reckoned. Hastily throwing a couple of turns of rope around one of my legs, I let myself drop hand-over-hand to the rock below. From that point I could see that the remaining distance would be over steep, sandstone slopes with few footholds anywhere. Playing out the rope as I went I began a series of zig-zags only to find that my momentum increased as I descended. When about 10 feet from the bottom the rope slipped from my grasp and I landed in a heap at the bottom."

Fortunately for today's hiker, the descent on iron rings is nowhere near as harrowing as it once was. Just remember the old rock climber's adage: secure three limbs before moving the fourth.

The story about the naming of Hole-in-the-Wall is easy to envision as you encounter the twisted maze of red rock. As the legend goes, in the 1880s, a couple of ranch hands from nearby Dominguez Ranch were seaching for some stray cattle, and they came upon a pair of Indians who were leading a few cattle. Suspecting them of stealing their stock, the ranch hands chased the Indians into a canyon, which they thought was a dead-end. To their amazement, the Indians scrambled up the rocks in the lower canyon, and then disappeared—seemingly right into the blank wall. The men concluded the Indians must have found or created a hole in the wall.

Enjoy exploring the volcanic rock formations known as rhyolite, a crystallized form of lava. The holes provide frames for taking silly photographs. You might spot any number of raptors circling overhead: golden eagles, hawks and owls.

Hole-in-the-Wall is not the only place in this area with a colorful name. Banshee is named not for the shrieking elves of the Scottish Highlands, but for the sounds said to be heard here at night that resemble their cries. Horned owls and the sound of the wind whistling through the holes make a quiet night in the canyon unlikely.

Don't miss a hike through Banshee Canyon that leads to Wild Horse Canyon. Follow Banshee to its opening, then turn north follow the wash and pick your way cross-country to the indistinct trail leading northward. The trail climbs gently onto a low mesa that offers good views of Wild Horse Mesa to the left, and desert varnish-covered rock formations on the right.

Continue northward through a magnificent devil's garden filled with yucca, cholla, beavertail, barrel and prickly pear cactus. In the springtime, the cactus bloom spreads bright yellow and hot pink across the canyon.

As you near the end of the canyon, enjoy the view of the juniper-filled basin to the north, the mountains and mesas in every direction. If you continued northward, you would reach Mid Hills, but the hike between the two campgrounds is best done north to south. There's more than a 1,000-foot elevation difference between Mid Hills and Hole-in-the-Wall, and the hike is simply more fun when it's downhill all the way.

CHAPTER FOURTEEN

Lanfair Valley

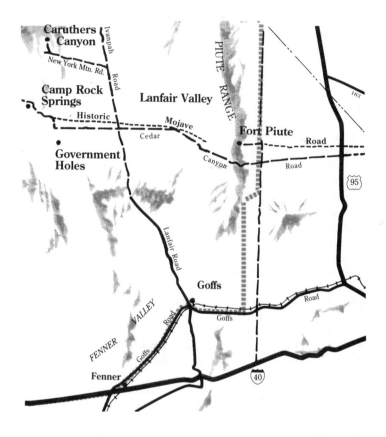

DRIVING NORTH ON Lanfair Road from the small town of Goffs, you'll view a wide-open landscape of yucca and Joshua trees, with several mountains ranges in the distance. There's hardly a trace of the turn-of-the-century farming community that once stood here. The intersection of Cedar Canyon and Lanfair Roads was once the entrance to a small town populated by farmers and ranchers.

Homesteaders descended on the Mojave Desert during America's period of westward expansion, from 1860 through 1920. Not coincidentally, this was also a period of particularly wet weather in the Mojave. Cattle ranchers and farmers settled in with varied success, but they gave their new homesteads optimistic names such as Golden, Surprise and Superior.

Edwin Lanfair lent his name to the area originally named Paradise Valley after he settled in 1910. The valley's first successful farmer, Lanfair raised bumper crops of wheat and barley in the desert. His good fortune attracted other homesteaders who flocked to the area; some managed to grow enough produce to sell it in markets in Needles.

The shortage of water was an ever-present problem in the valley. Although two wells were eventually established by Lanfair, many homesteaders chose instead to transport their water from Government Holes, a dozen miles to the west. The continued mild, wet weather held, encouraging them to stay, despite the difficulty of eking out a living in the middle of the desert.

The ranchers who had lived in the area were unhappy with the burgeoning homestead community. They refused to sell the farmers even a drop of water. Long-simmering disputes over land and water rights developed between small farmers, ranchers and big cattlemen. They finally erupted in a Wild-West shoot-out at Government Holes.

Months before, a few homesteaders infuriated Rock Springs cattle ranchers when they purchased several head of sheep and cattle and began grazing them on the open range. Considering the act an infringement on their grazing rights, the ranchers eventually fenced off the water supply at Government Holes, the only dependable source of water available to the homesteaders.

The already tense situation became even worse when hot tempers flared between a former Rock Springs man turned- homesteader Matt Burts, a convicted train robber, and J.W. Robinson, the newly hired Rock Springs foreman, known for his shady, violent past.

When Burts offered to drive his friend R.L. Fulton to work, the radiator of his car began leaking. He nursed the vehicle toward Government Holes, where he intended to get some water. When he called out and announced his plan, Robinson told him to go ahead; when Burt finished filling the radiator, he approached the cabin to talk with Robinson. Shots rang out and when Fulton ran in, he found both men mortally wounded. Apparently, Robinson had ambushed Burts, who then pulled his gun and killed Robinson as he fell to the floor.

This 1925 duel was the final blow for the homestead community of Lanfair Valley. Two years prior to the incident at Government Holes, the Nevada Southern Railroad abandoned the station it had established in Lanfair Valley to handle the ores shipped from local mines. A decline in mining activity and a debilitating strike were the reasons cited for the closure.

Ranch in the Ivanpah district, circa 1880.

The end of the railroad, the onset of a period of increasingly arid weather, and the homesteaders' loss of confidence in the community after the violence at Government Holes all contributed to the end of the settlement. In 1926, the store and post office were closed.

Although ranchers still graze their herds in Lanfair Valley, few traces remain of the earlier settlers. A windmill here, a water tank there, and some ruins are all that remain of the the original settlements—reminders of the dreams of optimistic homesteaders whose hopes were dashed by the harsh realities of desert life.

Fort Piute

Fort Piute is nestled in the Piute Range, with a grand view all the way to Arizona, and next to the dependable water source at Piute Creek. It's easy to imagine the despair felt by the tiny contingent of soldiers assigned to this desolate spot.

Hike to the ruins of Fort Piute and travel back in time.

Fort Piute is located east of Lanfair Valley, at the southern end of the Piute Mountains. It was established in the 1860s as one of a chain of five outposts along the Government Road—stretching from Fort Mojave in Nevada to Camp Cady to the west—to provide a military presence in the desert, and to protect pioneer travelers on their westward journeys.

As was the case in much of the West, Indians resisted the intrusion of settlers on their tribal lands. There were frequent attacks on westbound settlers and mail wagons traveling the route from Prescott, Arizona, to Los Angeles.

The military escorts presumably protected the travelers, but the conditions at the outpost were intolerable for many soldiers at Fort Piute. Desertion was a regular occurrence, and the outpost was officially staffed by just 18 men of the Company "D" 9th Infantry Division from 1867 to 1868.

In the late 1800s, Fort Piute was described by visitor Elliot Coues as "a Godforsaken Botany Bay of a place—the meanest I ever saw for a military station." It's doubtful that many who visit this tiny, lonely Army outpost would disagree.

Originally named Fort Beale, for Edward F. Beale who led his camels through this area, the outpost was renamed Fort Piute in 1866. Today the small, primitive installation lies in ruins; its thick rock and mortar walls have been weathered and crumbled to a height of just two or three feet. The stone outlines of the original buildings delineate three connecting rooms that served as a tiny living quarters, corral and cookhouse.

Near the fort stands an early example of an Army make-work project that dates back more than a century. The popular tale is that the rock wall situated above Piute Creek was constructed by Army troops who were then instructed to tear it down and rebuild it on the same site. No doubt the project kept several soldiers busy for some time.

There are many petroglyphs located near Fort Piute—evidence of the presence of native people long before the outpost was established. Soldiers who passed through the area in the mid-1800s sketched their versions of the artifacts. Look for them and try to determine the meaning and significance of the interesting shapes and figures. Although they have been studied extensively, they are still not completely understood.

The Old Mojave Road

The Mojave Road was a major trade and transportation route between Arizona and the coast. One look at the rough road gives you an idea of the hardships experienced by the pioneers who passed this way 130 years ago. Piute Hill, on the Mojave Road, was said to be among the most feared obstacles of the Westward crossing. In 1867, Brigadier General James F. Rusling described the ordeal of crossing the hill as "the worst climb I encountered in my entire tour across the continent."

As they pushed and pulled and dragged their heavy wagons up the rocky hills, the weary travelers prodded their oxen to keep them moving. Sometimes they were forced to wedge lumber beneath the wheels as they struggled to prevent the wagons from rolling backward, pouring every ounce of strength into creating forward momentum. Their taxing effort finally got them over the treacherous pass. But as the pioneers worked and maneuvered their cumbersome loads, the wagon wheels slowly ground into the surface of the rock. Over time, the wagonloads carved deep ruts in the solid rock; these ruts are still visible on Piute Hill today. They remain as vivid reminders of the difficulties faced—and overcome—by determined men and women of another age.

Today, four-wheel-drive enthusiasts still use the Mojave Road but they take a slightly different route than early travelers. Now the road is more apt to be seen as recreation, not desperation.

Former Scenic Area Manager John Bailey points out ruts made by wagons traveling the Mojave Road.

Piute Valley and Piute Creek

The overgrown willows and cottonwoods lining Piute Creek pose a challenge for hikers.

From the intersection of Lanfair and Cedar Canyon Roads, drive east on the utility road 9.5 miles. Turn north on small dirt road that leads to a pole corral and park.

(Fort Piute is also accessible from the east, but it's four-wheel drive access only. Turn west off US 95 at milepost 75, north of Goffs Road. Use caution; the road is rough and potholed.)

Begin your trek by heading toward two posts to the east. Pass through a cattleguard fence, and head cross-country up Piute Hill and meet up with the Old Mojave Road just over the crest of the hill. From atop the hill, pause to take in the view. Table Mountain can be seen directly to the west, and in the north are Castle Peaks.

As you continue hiking east into Piute Valley, you'll note the nearly solid rock surface. This common desert formation is known as caliche, a conglomerate rock with a limestone foundation. Because it is nearly impenetrable, it acts as a barrier to rainfall, forcing the water to run off, rather than percolating into the water table below.

You have the option of following the trail cairns down to the wash or on the upper slope of the hill; the trails rejoin later. Continue downhill to the wash of Piute Creek.

Walk down the loose, sandy trail to the creek, which is a lovely picnic stop. Continue up the trail to the east, which leads to the ruins of the fort. A marker provides some information about the history of "Fort Pah Ute, 1867-68." Remember, the ruins, like all cultural resources in the East Mojave, are protected by law.

153

The only perennial stream in the East Mojave, Piute Creek is an oasis-like area where cottonwoods, willows and sedges flourish. Bighorn sheep frequently visit this watering site, as do a large number of birds. Indians once farmed pumpkins, corn, melons and other crops near the spring, and others diverted its flow and irrigated their fields.

Access to the water and the rich hunting and farming land of the surrounding area was once hotly disputed between local Indian tribes. This idyllic location was also the location of a series of horrifying battles between Indians and westward travelers, including soldiers and trappers. In 1827, Jedediah Smith and the remainder of his party holed up near here after 10 of his fellow trappers were killed, and in 1859 at least 20 men died in a bloody confrontation.

In more recent years, enterprising George Irwin established a turkey ranch near here; a few remains of the ranch can still be seen east of the creek.

Although the creek has been a dependable source of water for centuries, the water is no longer safe to drink. Don't be tempted, or you'll pay for it later.

Cactus stands and cultural artifacts— virtually undisturbed in this isolated section of the East Mojave.

The steep and rugged New York Mountains—one of the most popular East Mojave destinations.

CHAPTER FIFTEEN

New York Mountains

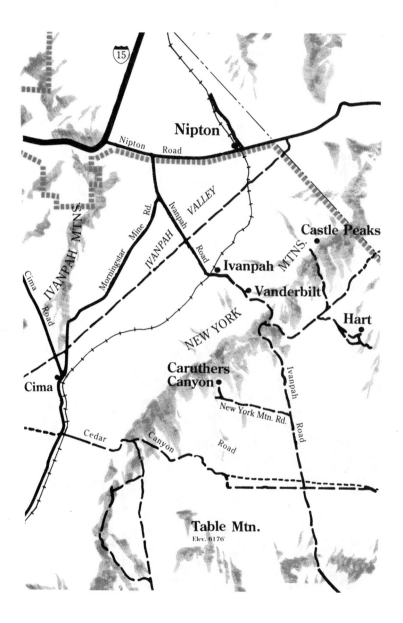

New York Mountains Area

BOUNDED BY CIMA ROAD on the west and Cedar Canyon to the south, is the New York Mountains area. The granite peaks of the New York range are the most prominent feature in the northeast corner of the East Mojave. This is a land of mountaintops and canyons, unique botanical communities and interesting geology. But it's the human history that also makes this section of the desert particularly appealing.

Today's visitors will note several man-made features—signs and fences, homesteads and watertanks—clues that miners and ranchers make a living off this land. But few clues remain—mostly abandoned mines and ghost town ruins far up into the hills—that tell the story of the way of life that once boomed here. The hills come alive, however, with a reading of the colorful tales of the area's bad guys and lawmen, chivalrous duels and lost mines.

All aboard! Everyone who lived and worked in the East Mojave counted on the railroad.

Vanderbilt, Barnwell and Lanfair have faded away, but back in 1920 were big enough for regularly scheduled rail service.

WESTWARD First Class **91** MIXED Leave Monday and Friday Only A M 8.30					TIME TABLE NO. 54 May 5, 1926 STATIONS		EASTWARD Second Class **92** MIXED Arrive Monday and Friday Only P M 2.40
	166	W Y		116.2	COFFS 9.1	P	
f 8.55	5		9.1	116.8	VONTRIGGER 3.7	o	f 2.10
f 9.05		11.4		106.6	BLACKBURN 3.2	o	f 2.00
f 9.15	3	18.2		105.6	LANFAIR 6.2	o	f 1.50
f 9.35	7	31.2		112.5	LEDGE 2.6	o	f 1.28
f 9.43	3	31.2		116.8	PURDY 4.7	156.4	f 1.20
*10.00	16	Y	31.4	52.8	BARNWELL 5.9	B	* 1.05
f10.15	5		38.4	52.8	HITT 5.0	132.0	12.45
f10.30	19		43.4	52.8	JUAN 11.7	132.0	12.30
11.00 A M	29	W Y	61.1		SEARCHLIGHT	DP	12.01 P M
	18	Y	33.5	53.1	BARNWELL 4.7	156.4	B
	6		34.2		VANDERBILT 4.2	156.4	
			38.4		IVANPAH		

Vanderbilt

Gold miners who staked claims here in 1890 dubbed their new town Vanderbilt in honor of the wealthy industrialist Commodore Cornelius Vanderbilt. The miners figured the name would bring fame, fortune and prestige—not to mention a good deal of luck. By the turn of the century, the town's population reached 3,000 and boasted a weekly newspaper, several general stores and saloons, a few boarding houses and a number of social clubs. It takes some imagination to conjure up the vision, but the citizens of this one-time boomtown created their own theatrical company, orchestra and even a literary society.

One of the area's movers and shakers was Isaac Blake, who made his fortune with Standard Oil and purchased a smelting plant in Needles and interests in several area mining projects. In 1892, he began construction of the Nevada Southern, a private railroad in the Providence Mountains. A few years later, he built the California and Eastern Railroad, a narrow gauge line that ran between Vanderbilt and Ivanpah Dry Lake. The railroads enabled miners to ship their ore to waiting markets, and the town prospered.

159

After an initial boom, when the mines—like Gold Bar, Gold Bronze Mine and Boomerang—combined to produce more than two million turn-of-the-century dollars worth of gold, the town's prosperity waned. The low-grade gold required extensive and expensive processing. Mine operators soon realized they could not turn a profit when they considered high production costs.

Townspeople, always concerned about the unreliable water supply, were faced with the fact that gold mining was no longer dependable either. As was the case with so many other boomtowns, Vanderbilt soon became yet a ghost town, its buildings and the possessions of its former residents taken over by time. Today, only a few ruins of the old buildings remain here.

Manvel (Barnwell)

Another small town, originally known as Manvel (later Barnwell), was once located four miles south of Vanderbilt. Not a mining town, but a railroad camp, the late 19th-Century settlement was a major drop-off point for products shipped from Needles and Goffs on their way to the small mining camps and settlements nearby—including the then-tiny town of Las Vegas, Nevada. When the railroad was bypassed by the large San Pedro, Los Angeles and Salt Lake Railroad, the town quietly folded.

The last of the town's original settlers was Dick Diamond, a former slave who moved to Manvel in the 1890s. Diamond, who lived to the age of 100, died in 1950. As the story goes, for the sixty years he lived in Manvel, Diamond proudly displayed a lithograph of Abraham Lincoln on his living room wall, explaining to all his visitors that it was Lincoln who had made him a free man. Like many other mining towns, Barnwell has been reduced to ruins.

Hart

The town of Hart is still found on some modern maps. Blink and you'll miss it. Hart was established when gold was discovered in 1907. Less than a year later, the town had a newspaper, two hotels and eight saloons, a small population of miners and several mines, none of which recouped initial investment costs.

An old miner, Stoney Feetham, who operated out of Hart, is said to have found a remarkably rich vein of gold in the hills not far out of town. Greedily, he stuffed his pockets, the bags carried by his burro, and every other container with as much gold-filled ore as he could carry. He quickly hatched a plan to hide his booty and return to the site to mine it in earnest. Back in Hart, Feetham told no one of his discovery. When he went back to mine the vein again, he couldn't even find a trace of it. When they finally found out about his so-called vein, Feetham was ridiculed by his friends, who derisively referred to it as the "Lost Mine of the Clouds." For the rest of his life, Old Stoney searched for "his" gold. He never found it.

Mining camp, New York Mountains.

The mines were no longer productive by the time the town was virtually destroyed by fire in 1910, but a few hopefuls hung on until the last

mine finally closed in 1918. In the town's later years, the pressures of economic losses, along with the stresses of living in an isolated, harsh environment, began to take their toll.

In 1913, the town was a site of an impassioned argument that ended in a shoot-out between two miners who were fighting over the attentions of a local woman. One shot the other, then, feeling immediately remorseful about his deed, sought medical attention for his dying rival, and turned himself in to the sheriff at Goffs. The gunman was jailed, the other man died.

Fenced-off areas, heavy machinery, and trucks rumbling through the New York Mountains are clues to visitors that mining and milling continue today among many of the sites where prospectors once trudged, loaded with pickaxe and hopeful hearts. But today's operations are high-tech big businesses run by international conglomerates. Modern processing methods substitute chemicals for manpower, tons of earth moved for smaller-scale work. Hardly romantic, but sometimes quite profitable.

The New York Mountains

The mountains range in elevation from about 5,400 to more than 7,000 feet. New York Mountain Peak rises to a height of 7,532, one of the highest points in the East Mojave. The steep range of granite and limestone also features a number of volcanic formations, including walls of lava on Pinto Mountain (elevation 6,144 feet). Castle Peaks, jagged red-colored volcanic spires composed of andesite are quite prominent, even when viewed from Fort Piute, across Lanfair Valley, and from other faraway locales.

Some three hundred plant species have been counted on the slopes and in the canyons of the New York Mountains. Botanists have even discovered several species of ferns here, some of which are found nowhere else. In addition to these individual species, there are some unique botanical communities in the New York Mountains area; experts refer to them as disjuncts. The isolated communities of pinyon pine and white fir, along with coastal chaparral plants grew throughout this area during wetter times. As the weather became more arid, the coastal and mountain ecosystems were "stranded," and they managed to survive to this day. A white fir forest stands near the top of New York Mountain; pinyon pine and juniper woodlands are found above 4,000 feet throughout the area; a coastal chaparral community thrives at Caruthers Canyon.

Caruthers Canyon

Located just a short hike off New York Mountain Road, Caruthers Canyon is a quiet retreat nestled in the New York Range. Hikers, bird-watchers and botany buffs enjoy exploring Caruthers Canyon. It's a popular campsite, although no facilities are located here.

This desert canyon features a thriving community of coastal chaparral. You would expect to see its live oaks, manzanita, yerba santa, ceonothus and coffee berry in the Santa Monica Mountains— not in the middle of the desert. But the botanical islands stranded here many years ago still manage to cling tenaciously to life. The canyon's chaparral community is joined by an assortment of cactus and at higher elevations, a woodland community of pinyon pine and juniper trees.

Great bird-watching opportunities abound in the woodland

Abandoned mine shafts abound in the East Mojave like this one in Caruthers Canyon. Contemplate the dreams that built them, but don't venture into the dark, unsafe passages.

community: Enthusiasts may spot Western tanager, gray-headed junco, yellow breasted chat, and a number of raptors, including golden eagles, prairie falcons and red-tailed hawks.

To hike into this unique canyon, take the long-abandoned dirt road that leads through a rocky basin and into a historic gold mining area. As you walk up-canyon through a wonderland of giant red granite boulders that line the trail, you'll be treated to excellent views of Table Mountain and the surrounding East Mojave. At the end of the trail are a small stand of white fir and the remains of an abandoned gold mine—both intriguing reminders of days gone by. Stay a safe distance from the gold mine; the abandoned shafts are dangerous.

Pinyon pines, great granite boulders and clean fresh air.

CHAPTER SIXTEEN

Cima Dome Area

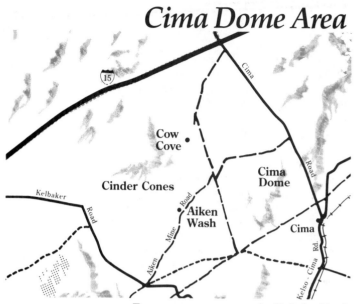

THE TRIANGLE BOUNDED by Kelbaker Road on the west, and Cima/Kelso Cima Road, which slants southwest to northwest, is a unique section of the East Mojave. Its distinctive volcanic geology, cultural artifacts and botanical characteristics combine to make this area of particular interest to desert visitors.

During the late 1960s, this area was slated for inclusion in the state park system, but high construction costs for improvements—roads, campgrounds, facilities—led decision-makers to drop the site from consideration. Those who appreciate the wide-open spaces and wild quality of this area are no doubt grateful that it wasn't "improved."

Access to the heart of this area is on dirt roads; although some high-clearance passenger vehicles might get you there, pickup trucks and heavy-duty vehicles are safer and more appropriate. Aiken Mine Road, the main road through the area, is usually well-graded, but it can be soft in spots. On your tour of the Cima Dome area, be sure to visit the tiny Cima General Store and Post Office.

Cima Dome

Located just west of Cima Road, 25 miles due east of Baker, is the unique geologic formation known as Cima Dome. The almost-perfectly symmetrical dome is a geologic rarity, the most symmetrical natural dome feature in the United States. (If you have any doubt, take a look at the area's USGS topographical map and study the near-concentric contour lines.) This mass of once-molten monzonite, a granite-like rock, was uplifted by volcanic action; over thousands of years it has been extensively eroded. The formation now covers some 75 square miles and rises nearly 1,500 feet above the 4,000-foot desert floor.

The rock outcroppings found here, particularly in the area of Teutonia Peak, are composed of the same type of rock that forms the distinctive, handsome rock outcroppings at Joshua Tree National Park to the south. Naturally, they are attractive to rock scramblers and rock-climbers. The remains of an old silver mine can still be seen at Teutonia Peak.

East Mojave visitors are frequently confused about Cima Dome. Cima Dome is a place you drive on, not to. It's not a geologic formation you can view up-close; since the Dome slopes so gently, it's best viewed from a distance. The northernmost point at Mid Hills campground offers the best vantage point of the Dome, although it can also be viewed from Interstate 15, near Baker.

The Cima Dome area hosts the world's largest Joshua tree forest.

Joshua Tree Forest

Once proposed as a state park, the Joshua Tree forest has long been a favorite attraction.

Atop Cima Dome is the site of the world's largest, tallest and densest Joshua tree forest. The most oft-repeated observation about the Joshua tree was made by 19th-Century explorer John C. Frémont who called it "the most repulsive tree in the vegetable kingdom." Admittedly, the charms of a Joshua tree forest are unlike those of a stand of redwoods, but true desert rats consider the spiky tree a handsome feature of this dry land.

Yucca brevifolia, the Joshua tree, is actually a member of the lily family. Nothing about the plant gives a clue to its botanical bloodlines. Not its stiff stalks, shaggy trunk or towering height of 20 to 30 feet. This distinctive symbol of the Mojave Desert thrives at an elevation of about 4,000 feet. Although the trees are the most visible sign of life here, they shelter a thriving underbrush community of cholla and associated plants and animals.

The number of natural springs in the area attracts a variety of birds, including hawks, quail, and the loggerhead shrike. Cima Dome offers breeding habitat for the Bendire's Thrasher, and it's one of only two places the California Desert where the Gilded Common Flicker lives (Clark Mountain, fifteen miles north is the other). Other animals include an assortment of reptiles and small mammals.

Cinder Cones

This 25,600-acre area has been designated a National Natural Landmark. Consisting of 32 volcanic formations, the cones are thought to date back 10 million years. These remnants of once-active vulcanism in the East Mojave create an interesting, almost eerie red-black moonscape.

Legend has it that the Apollo astronauts trained on this moon-like surface in preparation for their historic 1969 lunar landing. But officials deny that such maneuvers ever occurred. As you look out on this landscape, however, you can easily imagine the space-suited explorers bounding around on this moon-like surface, with the Cinder Cones in the background.

Neil Armstrong may not have taken even one small step for man on this volcanic field, but it does attract geologists from all over the world. The composition of the rock is said to be denser than anywhere on earth; it provides scientists with important information about geologic processes below the earth's surface.

The Aiken Mine has mined one of the cinder cones since the 1960s; the lightweight reddish material has literally been hauled away by the ton—it eventually ends up lining gardens and walkways of suburban homes and offices. Although some environmentalists consider the mine site a blight on the land, visitors are often fascinated by the opportunity to peer into the inside of a cinder cone.

Outside the entrance to lava tube.

Ropy strands of pahoehoe lava remain from long ago volcanic eruptions.

Cow Cove

Located about five miles off Aiken Mine Road, Cow Cove is an outstanding petroglyph site that provides a glimpse into the culture of the past. Although little is known about the figures carved into these rocks, much is speculated. Today's visitor may imagine and attribute all sorts of meanings to the drawings that may be thousands of years old.

As you hike near the rocks, you'll view abstract figures and others that appear to have more literal meanings. Remember that these cultural artifacts, along with all other cultural resources in the

East Mojave, are protected by Federal law. The Archeological Resources Protection Act of 1979 states that no person may "excavate, remove, damage, alter or deface any archeological resource." Fines for ignoring the law range up to $20,000 for a first offense, up to five years in jail for repeat offenders. Enjoy the site, but leave it undisturbed. Remember: The past belongs to the future, but only the present can preserve it.

The petroglyphs of Cow Cove fascinate us. What is the significance of these figures?

Aiken Wash

Located just off Aiken Mine Road, south of the Cinder Cones, is Aiken Wash, a favorite desert destination among those who enjoy getting off the beaten path. Also called Willow Wash for the large collection of large willow trees that thrives here, this wash runs through one of the most scenic areas

Inside the lava tube bathed in the strong light.

of the East Mojave. The willows, Joshua trees and Mojave yucca, combined with the views of the nearby Cinder Cones and the solid black wall of basalt rock cut by the wash, make it a particularly memorable location. The willow-lined dry streambed is a lovely place to hike, especially in the springtime, when fragrant desert lavender is in full bloom.

The availability of surface water, the large assortment of edible cactus, and the abundance of trees at this site made it attractive to prehistoric people. There is evidence of human habitation in many cave-like areas near the wash, and many petroglyphs can be seen here. Like those at Cow Cove, five miles away, the cultural artifacts are protected by law.

Lava Tube

For a memorable experience, locate and explore the lava tube located in the cinder cone area. (Ask for exact directions: access can be confusing in this area where landmarks are indistinct.) During a long-ago volcanic eruption when swift-moving lava flowed over the land, the lava tube was formed when the inner flow cooled more quickly than the outer flow. Today, the resulting cave-like formation appears to be a great hole in the earth. Someone has placed a somewhat rickety ladder in the tube to facilitate climbing down into it; use caution as you maneuver into it. Making your way through the underground tube requires some bending and stretching; at one point explorers must flatten on the ground and squeeze through a small opening to enter the great cave.

Bring a flashlight to explore the cave's nooks and crannies. The cool, dark underground area is a welcome retreat from the often-scorching outdoor temperatures and unrelenting sunlight; you're likely to spot bats or owls that inhabit the cave. Enjoy the unique setting, especially the beams of light that flood sections of the cave.

CHAPTER SEVENTEEN

Clark Mountain

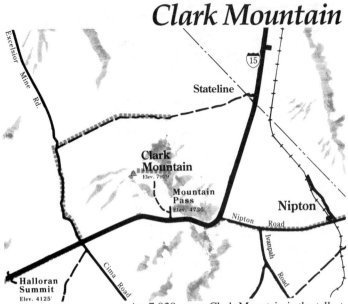

AT 7,929 FEET, Clark Mountain is the tallest peak in the East Mojave Desert. Situated in the Clark Range, the rugged mountain is one of the few places in the East Mojave to be covered with a relict stand of white fir trees.

This handsome environment has been inhabited for thousands of years. Chemehuevi, Piute and Mohaves lived here. Archeologists have discovered a number of artifacts, including petroglyphs, rock shelters and rock alignments in the Clark Mountains. They have also found a number of large ash-filled pits where native people once roasted agave for food. Some experts speculate that native people may have considered the mountain a spiritually significant site.

Clark Mountain has much to offer today's visitor in the way of scenic value and a diverse environment, but is virtually inaccessible except in a four-wheel drive vehicle. The road to the mountain is dirt; road conditions can be quite variable and it should not be attempted in any vehicle except one suited to traveling on questionable roads.

Tallest peak in the East Mojave, 7,929-foot-high Clark Mountain.

Access to Clark Mountain is off I-15 at Mountain Pass. There you'll view the Molycorp Mine, a long-established rare-earth mine. The dirt road just past the one-room elementary school is the main access to Clark Mountain. It leads through a land of Joshuas and rises into a land of junipers and pinyon pine.

At the end of the road, you'll find a handsome picnic area, complete with barbeque pits, picnic tables and a volleyball court, all nestled in a pinyon pine forest. The facilities were established here by Molycorp many years ago. The company formerly held its annual family picnic at the Clark Mountain site.

Today, the spot is a lovely place to picnic, or to use as a jumping-off spot for further exploration of the Clark Mountains. The area supports a number of plant communities, which provides varied habitat for a number of animal species. A good-sized population of bighorn sheep thrive here, as do raptors and several snakes and lizards.

Clark's pinyon pine shaded picnic area, a peaceful retreat.

Mining at Clark Mountain

Clark Mountain has been mined for more than a century; it produced more than four million 19th-Century dollars worth of silver, along with significant amounts of gold, copper and several other rare, precious and semi-precious materials.

In less than 15 years Clark Mountain's Lizzie Bullock Mine produced several million dollars worth of silver. The mine was played out by 1885.

On the the slopes of Clark Mountain is the site of the town of Ivanpah, which was established soon after three lucky propectors discovered a rich vein of silver in the mountain. A short-lived boomtown, the first town in the East Mojave, was founded in 1869; in 1875 its population was 500, mostly miners. By the end of the century, the town was abandoned. Only a few ruins of the fifteen buildings that once stood here still can be seen today.

Clark Mountain is the subject of one of the more colorful and enticing Mojave mining tales—the Lost River of Gold. A 1920s miner, Earl Dorr, tried to convince investors to finance his discovery in Crystal Cave—a 3,000-foot deep river through the mountain, its sands filled with gold.

Dorr managed to gain the backing of several wealthy Los Angeles speculators. He struck a rich vein, all right, but it was zinc, not gold. The Lost River has never been found, and today the mine is privately owned. The notion, however, of a Lost River of Gold continues to fascinate and inspire imaginations to this day.

California fan palms mark the entrance of the desert oasis created by Doc Springer.

CHAPTER EIGHTEEN

Soda Springs / Zzyzx

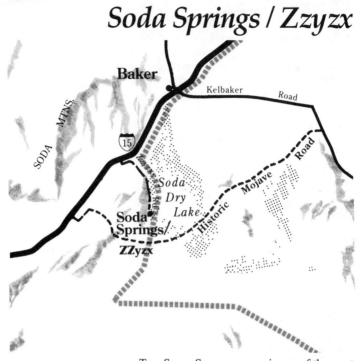

THE SODA SPRINGS AREA is one of the most fascinating places in the East Mojave. Because of its year-round supply of fresh water, it has long been a stopping point for westbound travelers, settlers and desert dwellers.

Soda Dry Lake is the largest playa in the East Mojave. The term 'dry lake,' however, is a misnomer; the lake's surface is often muddy and wet. It is located just east of the Mojave River Sink, where the Mojave begins to flow underground.

Located six miles southwest of Baker, about 60 miles northeast of Barstow, Soda Springs has a long and colorful history. Native people have lived here for thousands of years; their tools, cairns and cleared areas, known as "sleeping circles," date back to the Pleistocene Period, 8,000 B.C. Their descendants left archeological evidence of continued occupation through the mid-1800s.

As was the case throughout the west, when settlers, trappers and explorers traveled through, there were clashes with the Indians who were tied to their ancestral homelands. In 1860, the U.S. Army established an outpost at Soda Springs known as "Hancock's Redoubt." Intended to escort travelers along the Mojave Road and the U.S. Mail carriers, the outpost was described as ". . . a series of breastworks and corrals . . . constructed of mud and willow-brush." De-commissioned after 1868, the outpost became a commercial rest stop—known variously as "Soda Station" and "Shenandoah Camp"—for travelers.

The Tonopah and Tidewater Railroad, which ran north from Ludlow to Silver Lake, was built by Francis "Borax" Smith in 1905. The railroad was created to transport iron ore and passengers; to serve the needs of travelers, a station was built in Soda Springs. It lasted less than a year, and closed in 1908. The railroad, however, continued to run until the early '40s, when the tracks were torn up and used as scrap metal as part of the war effort.

Zzyzx Mineral Springs and Health Resort

Soda Springs then entered a colorful new era that was to last some 30 years, from 1944 through 1974. Thanks to the efforts of Dr. Curtis Springer, Soda Springs became much more than an oasis. It was turned into a resort that promised health to its thousands of visitors and financial supporters. Known as Zzyzx Mineral Springs and Health Resort, Springer's development in the middle of the desert was established on the basis of mining claims registered with the government.

Springer may have gotten the idea for the health resort and mining claim from reading comments of travelers through Soda Springs. Lt. Robert Williamson wrote in 1853 of ". . . several fine springs, slightly brackish but not unpalatable."

Wearing his trademark white suit, Doc Springer always greeted his guests with a smile and a wave.

The next year, Lt. Amiel Weeks Whipple wrote, "the dry bed of the lake covered with efflorescent salts, probably sulphate of soda." But he wasn't the first to come up with the notion of using the water at Soda Springs for therapeutic purposes. In 1871, an article about Soda Springs appeared in the *San Bernardino Guardian*. "The boys have built for the use of the public a nice bathing place and invited us to take a bath while they are preparing dinner."

Springer posted office hours, but was said to be available at all times.

When Springer and his wife, Helen, arrived at Soda Springs in 1944, they described it as a "mosquito swamp." A few old buildings remained from previous ventures in the area, but the couple began to develop the place into a self-contained town unlike anything else in the Mojave.

A labor force recruited from L.A.'s Skid Row—each man was paid $10 per week—built the resort's extensive facilities. A 60-room hotel called The Castle, a dining hall, indoor baths and a large swimming pool shaped in the form of a cross were among the original projects. Springer broadcasted his daily religious programs from the radio station, and conducted services at the Zzyzx Community Church. Since there were no utility services, the entire development was self-contained and energy-efficient.

ZZYZX MINERAL SPRINGS

Our God Whom We Serve Is Able

The main road in the complex was named "Boulevard of Dreams," and for many years it was a fitting title. For thirty years, believers, health-seekers and the curious flocked to Zzyzx, lured by Springer's promises and products. "Our Hot Mineral Water baths, matchless climate and wonderful foods await you and remember a condition that has been coming on for years cannot be corrected in days so plan on staying with us long enough to give our facilities a chance to help," read a 1961 Springer brochure.

Although the self-proclaimed "old-time medicine man" never attached a fee to his concoctions or services, the donations poured in; "Freely you have received, as God makes possible, Freely Give," read the sign on a coin box placed on an exit table. It's been estimated that Springer's annual income ranged from $250,000 to $750,000.

Eventually, the powers-that-be began questioning Springer's methods and claims. He was charged with income tax evasion by the Internal Revenue Service; he was called "King of the Quacks" by the American Medical Association; he was convicted of false advertising by the Pure Food and Drug Administration; and his claim to the land and his Zzyzx facilities were finally confiscated by the Bureau of Land Management.

Despite a long, bitter court battle, including a lengthy article penned by Springer entitled "The Legal Rape of Zzyzx," he never returned to the resort after he was evicted in 1974; he died in 1985.

Doc Springer broadcasted his folksy philosophy on his radio show originating in Zzyzx.

The waters of Lake Tuendae; Doc Springer claimed the fish in the lake were in "health-conscious." He advised guests to bait their hooks with sun-dried raisins rather than salmon eggs.

Doc Springer marketed Antediluvian Herb Tea as an integral part of his Seven-day Cleansing Plan. He reminded the faithful, "Health is Wealth."

CALIFORNIA DESERT STUDIES
CONSORTIUM

Field research is often grueling work, but the rewards may be a new clue to the life of early man.

Soda Springs Today

An agreement between the Bureau of Land Management and the California State University established the Desert Studies Center at the former site of the Zzyzx resort. Some of Springer's buildings are still in use, although many have been rebuilt or improved; a new shower and kitchen have made the facility more comfortable for visitors.

Throughout much of the year, the Center offers classes to the public through State University Extension programs. Ranging from courses in astronomy to geology, archeology to botany, all feature desert experts and field trips. The Center is also available to students and faculty conducting research on selected desert topics.

Weekend tours of the facilities are conducted; contact the Desert Information Center in Barstow for details.

The rooms that once housed health seekers and sunworshipers now serve as dormitories for student researchers and scientists.

CHAPTER NINETEEN

Mojave River Basin

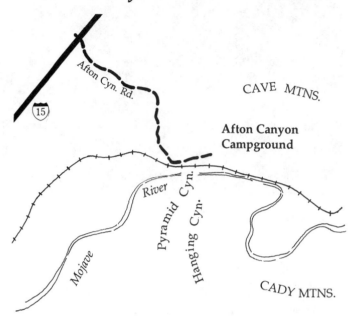

*Afton Canyon,
a geological
wonderland
sculpted by the
Mojave River.*

THE MOJAVE RIVER was formed thousands of years ago when the climate of the area was considerably wetter than it is today. When the San Gabriel and San Bernardino Mountains were being formed, the increased rainfall enhanced the size and power of the river. It deposited alluvial materials, wore down mountains, and cut gorges along its path. Afton Canyon, a beautiful, 600-foot deep canyon, was carved through the surrounding hills of solid granite. It's an impressive example of the power of the once-mighty Mojave.

The river emptied into the ancient Lake Manix, then meandered eastward into Lake Mojave (seen today as Soda and Silver dry lakes), and finally joined with the Amargosa River in Death Valley, both of which emptied into another ancient lake, Lake Manly. Changing weather patterns at the end of the Pleistocene, a few million

years ago, caused the lakes to dry up, and the river to become a relative trickle compared to its former size.

The banks of Lake Manix, along with the alluvial and bajada formations created by the flowing water, can be viewed from the northern edge of the East Mojave between Calico and Baker. One excellent vantage point is the Calico Early Man Archeological Site, where artifacts and the story of ancient dwellers make the land come alive.

Archeological evidence uncovered along the former banks of the river and ancient lakebeds indicates that not only did it support a large population of indigenous people, but it served as a trade route between present-day Arizona and the coast. The Mohave Indians left enormous piles of mussel shells, which they gathered on the shores of the lake. They also cultivated crops at the mouth of the Mojave River.

The Mohaves regularly came into contact with people who followed the river west. Cultural artifacts including pot shards, arrow points, choppers and scrapers, which were created by Mojave River people, have been found alongside ceramics, turquoise, bows and arrows fashioned by the Anasazi to the east. Further evidence of Anasazi

Mojave River during wetter times and climes was a river of considerable size. Even in today's arid climate, the Mojave manages to flow above ground in a few places, including Afton Canyon.

influence has been disovered at the turquoise mining site at Turquoise Mountain, north of Halloran Springs.

As the climate became more arid, the Mohave were forced to move toward the Colorado River to continue their way of life.

Today, the river is much less mighty than it once was. From the river's headwaters in the San Bernardino National Forest, at the Mojave River Forks Recreation Park and Flood Control Dam, the Mojave flows some 150 miles eastward, only a fraction of which is above ground. Just east of Afton Canyon, the river ends at the Mojave River Sink.

Afton Canyon

Father Garcés at his campfire.

Afton Canyon is one of the most conveniently located sites in the East Mojave Desert and a place that should not be missed. Take the Afton exit off Interstate 15, 33 miles east of Barstow; the graded 3-mile-long road leads to the campground in Afton Canyon. Park at the campground, being careful not to take a camp site.

The narrow, corridor-like Afton Canyon has been referred to as the "Grand Canyon of the Mojave." It is an eight-mile-long, narrow gorge with some sheer walls that rise 600 feet above the canyon floor. When he passed through the canyon in 1776, Fr. Garces wrote, "I went five leagues in a west-southwest direction and came to pass through the mountains. Streaks of different-colored minerals can be seen on the mountain-side. I named it "Sierra Pinta."

Fr. Garces was not the only historic figure to travel through Afton Canyon on his way from the

Colorado River to the Coast. Explorers Jedediah Smith, Kit Carson and John C. Frémont all journeyed through on their way west. William Adams Vale, who kept a journal during his trip through the desert, noted, "I walked down the canyon looking at caves and deep gorges in the mountains...Oh! What a country—there is some grand scenery in Cave Canyon."

Afton Canyon is one of the few places where the Mojave River runs year-round. The lush growth found here prompted Fr. Garces to write, "Here grows the wild grape; where there is much grass, also mesquite and the trees that grow the screw..." The dependable source of water supports a variety of plants including cottonwoods, willows, rabbit bush, smoketrees and grasses. A program is underway to remove the invasive tamarisk which threatens to choke out native species. The labor-intensive program, which requires cutting the tamarisk with a chain saw and the immediate application of an herbicide, will eventually result in a more oasis-like streamside community.

The plants that grow in the canyon provide shelter for many species of wildlife . Migratory birds are attracted to the site, as are several other

Best view of Afton Canyon may belong to the crew of the Union Pacific freight trains that rumble through the canyon; an equally fine view is available to hikers.

BLM Ranger Harold Johnson and others worked hard to rehabilitate Afton Canyon.

species of birds, including stream-frequenting herons, egrets, killdeer and ibis. California mud turtles, frogs, minnows and the Mohave chub live in the river or along the shore, and bighorn sheep travel down from the mountains to water in the area. The shy bighorn have been frightened off by the motorcycles that once took over this campground.

The Mojave Road in Afton Canyon has been re-routed in order to protect the sensitive riparian environment, and off-highway vehicles have been prohibited in the area due to significant damage that has been caused by irresponsible riders in such places as "Competition Hill," which can be seen on the approach to the canyon.

Railroad aficionados will delight in the number of passenger and freight trains that regularly pass through on the tracks that run the length of the canyon. The sight and sound of a mighty locomotive powering across gleaming trestles are practially unforgettable.

Afton Canyon features a number of smaller, side canyons which were formed from water draining out of the nearby Cady Mountains. It's been said that it would take you the rest of your life to

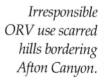

Irresponsible ORV use scarred hills bordering Afton Canyon.

Pyramid Canyon, one of Afton's scenic side Canyons.

find and explore all the little side canyons adjacent to Afton Canyon.

There are two main hikes in Afton Canyon: the hike up Pyramid Canyon, the major side canyon, and the hike through large Afton Canyon. You may also explore the side canyons to the north and south of Afton Canyon.

Pyramid Canyon, the deepest and largest of the side canyons, can easily be located and hiked. Cross the river under the first set of railroad trestles, just south of the campground. The scenic water-eroded formations of this canyon make it especially enjoyable. Raptors, including golden eagles and red-tailed hawks, can often be seen circling in this area. And rockhounds have long considered the canyon a rich site for gathering specimens, among them agates, geodes and Mexican sapphires.

Although there's no real trail up Pyramid Canyon, simply follow it to its rocky end, about two

miles from Afton Canyon. Improvise your route; the canyon is so wide that you may walk up one side and return to the trailhead on the opposite side.

The double trestle bridge just east of Cave Mountain marks the end of Afton Canyon. You may wish to return to the trailhead along the riverbed, rather than along the canyon wall.

If you're still feeling frisky after hiking through Pyramid Canyon, you may want to continue east through Afton Canyon. The water-cut, eight-mile-long canyon is an easy out-and-back hike; if you follow it to its end, it's a 16-mile round trip full-day hike. Gauge your distance accordingly. As you hike up-canyon, you'll view an old mine on the south wall of Afton Canyon. Although it appears to be an abandoned gold mine, the owner of the mine simply salted it with gold in order to sell worthless shares to unwitting investors.

Continuing east, you'll notice a number of side canyons situated on the north wall of Afton Canyon. These side canyons are most obvious when you look for the man-made culverts that have

From the canyon bottom, there are breathtaking views of Afton Canyon's water-eroded formations

Trains frequently rumble through Afton Canyon.

been placed to prevent further water erosion. At the culvert marked 192.99, is another canyon that features magnificently eroded shapes caused by thousands of years of wind and water.

At the culvert marked 194.65, take a flashlight to explore a fascinating cave/canyon that twists and turns; just when you think it ends, it turns once again and keeps going.

Camp Cady

Located off the I-15 Harvard Road exit, the Camp Cady area takes in part of the Mojave River floodplain where desert willow, cottonwoods and tamarisk flourish. Today, the land is owned and maintained by the California State Department of Fish and Game. The agency has plans to develop nature trails and a hunting reserve here, but now, hiking and bird-watching opportunities are available on a very limited, advance reservations only basis.

Camp Cady was once the westernmost of the string of tiny military forts established during the 1860s to protect westbound settlers and travelers. The post has been reduced to a crumbled corner of rocks chinked with mud nestled in a stand of willow trees.

Turn-of-the-century Greek immigrant, movie theatre magnate Alexander Pantages (of the famed Hollywood Pantages Theatre) built a thoroughbred

Since this photo was taken, Camp Cady has deteriorated markedly.

This boat was left high and dry when the Mojave River receded.

horse ranch and an enormous stable at this site. You can just imagine the sight of the pampered animals being put through their paces in this out-of-the way place.

A hike through this river floodplain reveals evidence that people lived throughout this area not so long ago: A ramshackle lean-to here, a thatched willow hut there, rusted-out abandoned vehicles and even a boat or two. Yes, boats; the Mojave River not so long ago had enough water to permit rowboats and motorboats to patrol this territory that in places resembles the setting for the classic movie "African Queen."

The resident bird population, along with the seasonal migratory short-term residents makes this a prime area for bird-watching. You may spot hawks, quail, owls and several other species; the endangered Mohave tui chub inhabits the ponds, as do frogs and mud turtles.

The Fish and Game staffers headquartered here are responsible for this 2,000-acre site, and for studying the bighorn sheep population in nearby mountains.

Desert adaptation may be no more remarkable than that of the forest, the jungle, the prairie or the sea, but it exposes life for what it is: conjured out of nothing. Here, from the nothing of drought, the nothing of life in flight, the nothing of sheer space, we miraculously are.

—Bruce Berger
The Telling Distance

PART IV

On Foot: Walking the East Mojave

CHAPTER TWENTY

Our Favorite Walks

Owl Canyon Trail

Owl Canyon Campground to Velvet Peak
5 miles round trip; 500-foot elevation gain

The designation on the map of "National Natural Landmark" is a tip-off, but nothing can prepare you for the sight of the spectacular series of colorful hills that comprise Rainbow Basin. Pink, white, orange, brown red, black and green sediments form the basin's rainbow-colored walls.

This superb place in the Calico Mountains is ideal for the hiker to sample the mountains, spectacular geology and rich historic record of the East Mojave Desert.

Some 15 million years ago, grasslands filled Rainbow Basin, which was populated by saber-toothed tigers, mastodons, camels, three-toed horses and even rhinoceros. Their fossil remains are encased in sedimentary rock that once formed a lakebed. As a result of intense geologic activity over the millenia, what was once at the bottom of the lake is now a series of folded, faulted, colorful hills.

Owl Canyon is one of three moderate hikes in Rainbow Basin. This canyon takes its name from the barn owls who live there. Hikers should be reasonably agile in order to tackle Owl Canyon Trail, because getting through canyon means scrambling over some boulders.

You could spend a pleasant weekend camping and hiking in Rainbow Basin. Stationed at Owl Canyon Campground is a campground host, who can provide hiking and touring tips.

Directions to trailhead: Follow Interstate 15 to Barstow, then join Highway 58 to Fort Irwin

Road, following it 5 miles. Turn west on dirt Fossil Road and proceed 3 miles to Owl Canyon Campground. The trail begins at the north end of the campground.

The walk: Follow the marked trail into Owl Canyon. Half a mile up-canyon look for a small cave on your right.

Colorful Owl Canyon—great for a short stroll, or a full weekend of camping and hiking.

Sandstone and siltstone, shale and volcanic debris are among the exposed rock visible to the hiker. The geologic formations en route are not only rainbow-colored but dramatic in shape. Particularly evident are massive downfolds geologists call synclines.

The canyon narrows for a time then opens up at its end into a multi-colored amphitheater. Velvet Peak is the high spot above the rocky bowl. Experienced hikers can scramble up the bowl's rocky ridges for fine views of Rainbow Basin and the vast East Mojave.

Afton Canyon Trail

Afton Campground to Pyramid Canyon
3 miles round trip

To Side Canyons
6 1/2 miles round trip

It's often called the Grand Canyon of the Mojave. High praise indeed, but then Afton Canyon is a very special place, a geological wonderland sculpted by the Mojave River.

Long ago, Afton Canyon was cut by outlet flow from a once-large body of water that geologists call Lake Manix. Some 15 to 75,000 years ago during a hot and much more humid climate, wildlife was abundant around the lake, which was shallow, but about 200 square miles in size. Turtles, shellfish, camels and antelope flourished. It's almost surreal to imagine a flock of pink flamingos, all standing on one leg, looking over a landscape that Great Inagua of the Bahamas than the Great American Desert.

The Mojave River, during these wetter times and climes, must have been a river of considerable size. Even in today's arid climate, the Mojave manages to flow either below ground or above for 145 miles across the desert.

The (relatively) well-watered Mojave River Valley has always served as a route of travel. During prehistoric times, Indians traveled the Mojave Trail from the California coast to the Colorado River. DeAnza's 1776 expedition passed through Afton Canyon on its way to Mission San Gabriel.

A half-century later, Jedediah Smith followed the Mojave and after getting a bit exasperated with the river's habit of disappearing underground for long stretches, called it, most aptly, "The Inconstant River." Kit Carson took the river route, as did John C. Frémont, who gave the Mojave its name.

Today, the best view of Afton Canyon and the path of the Mojave River may belong to the crew of the Union Pacific freight train that rumbles through the canyon. An equally fine view is available to hikers. You can explore large Afton Canyon, and its many side canyons, including the largest of them, Pyramid Canyon.

Directions to trailhead: From Interstate 15, 32 miles east of Barstow, take the Afton Canyon exit. Travel 3 miles southwest on a good dirt road to Afton Campground. Park at the campground, being careful not to take campsite space.

The walk: Before you follow the Mojave River through Afton Canyon, you might want to cross it from the campground, under the first set of railroad trestles, and head south through Pyramid Canyon. The largest and deepest of Afton's side canyons, 1 1/2-mile-long Pyramid Canyon is an easy stroll, and a good introduction to the fascinating geology of the area. The grand rock walls, cut away by the once-mighty Mojave, gradually narrow until you reach what looks to be a dead end. Experienced hikers may want to scramble to the top of this "dead end" for a grand view of the surrounding desert landscape.

Return to Afton Canyon and follow the river east. You'll notice a grand assemblage of desert riparian growth—native cottonwoods and willows, along with invasive tamarisk.

Continue hiking along the canyon's north wall for breathtaking views of water-eroded formations, and to explore the many side canyons. These canyons are, for the most part, indicated by culverts; look for those located at numbers 192.99 and 194.65. A flashlight is useful for finding your way.

Beyond this point the canyon widens and holds less interest for the hiker. Afton Canyon extends a few more miles to a double trestle bridge near Cave Mountain. For a different perspective of the canyon, consider returning via the river bottom.

Teutonia Peak Trail

Parking area to Cima Dome, Teutonia Peak
4 miles round trip

Cima Dome is one of the easier East Mojave sights to reach, but when you reach it, you're not really sure you've reached it. It's not a geologic formation you can view close-up: the Dome slopes so gently it's best viewed from a distance. What Gertrude Stein said of Oakland comes to mind: "There's no there there."

Two places to get "the big picture" of Cima Dome are from Mid Hills Campground and from I-15 as you drive southeast of Baker and crest a low rise.

The dome is a mass of once-molten monzonite, a granite-like rock. Over thousands of years it's been extensively eroded and now sprawls over some 75 square miles. It's over 10 miles in diameter.

Another distinctive feature of the dome is its handsome rock outcroppings—the same type found in Joshua Tree National Monument to the south. Rock climbers, rock scramblers and hikers love Cima's rock show.

The word to remember around Cima Dome is symmetry. A geological rarity, the almost perfectly symmetrical dome has been called the most symmetrical natural dome in the U.S.. If you take a look at the area's USGS topographical map and study Cima's near-concentric contour lines, you'll probably agree with this symmetry claim.

Symmetry is also a word used in conjuction with the area's other natural attraction: the Joshua tree. Botanists say Cima's Joshuas are more symmetrical than their cousins elsewhere in the Mojave

Symmetry may be in the eye of the beholder and hard to quantify, but without a doubt, Cima's Joshua trees are measurably tall—some more than 25 feet high—and several hundred years old.

Collectively, they form the world's largest and densest Joshua tree forest.

Here at an elevation of about 4,000 feet this distinct symbol of the Mojave desert truly thrives. Bring your camera!

This walk travels the famed Joshua tree forest, then visits Cima Dome, which rises 1,500 above the surrounding desert playas.

Directions to trailhead: The beginning of the trail is just off Cima Road, a scenic Back Country Byway that stretches seventeen miles from the Cima Road exit on Interstate 15 south to Cima. The signed trailhead is about 9 miles from I-15.

The walk: The mellow, two-mile Teutonia Peak Trail meanders through the Joshua tree forest and ascends to a lookout over Cima Dome. From the lookout, it's a quarter-mile scramble over rocks to the top of Teutonia Peak (elevation 5,755 feet).

The path is maintained by the San Gorgonio Chapter of the Sierra Club, which has plans to extend it farther over Cima Dome.

Caruthers Canyon Trail

Caruthers Canyon to Gold Mine
3 miles round trip; 400-foot elevation gain

Botanists call them disjuncts. Bureaucrats call them UPAs (Unusual Plant Assemblages). The more lyrical naturalists among us call them islands on the land.

By whatever name, the isolated communities of pinyon pine and white fir in the New York Mountains are very special places. Nearly three hundred plant species have been counted on the slopes of this range and in its colorfully named canyons—Cottonwood and Caruthers, Butcher Knife and Fourth of July.

Perhaps the most botanically unique area in the mountains, indeed in the whole East Mojave Desert, is Caruthers Canyon. A cool, inviting pinyon pine-juniper woodland stands in marked contrast to the sparsely vegetated sandscape common in other parts of the desert. The conifers are joined by oaks and a variety of coastal chaparral plants including manzanita, yerba santa, ceanothus and coffee berry. What is a coastal ecosystem doing in the middle of the desert?

Botanists believe that during wetter times such coastal scrub vegetation was quite widespread. As the climate became more arid, coastal ecosystems were "stranded" atop high and moist slopes. The botanical islands high in the New York Mountains are outposts of Rocky Mountains and coastal California flora.

Caruthers Canyon is a treat for the hiker. An abandoned dirt road leads through a rocky basin and into a historic gold mining region. Prospectors began digging in the New York Mountains in the 1860s and continued well into the 20th century. At trail's end are a couple of gold mine shafts.

The canyon's woodland offers great bird-watching. The western tanager, gray-headed junco, yellow-breasted chat and many more species are found here. Circling high in the sky are the raptors—golden eagles, prairie falcons and red-tailed hawks.

Directions to trailhead: From I-40, 28 miles west of Needles and some 117 miles east of Barstow, exit on Mt. Springs Road. You'll pass the tiny town of Goffs (last chance for provisions) and head north 27 1/2 miles on the main road, known variously as Ivanpah-Goffs Road or Ivanpah Road, to New York Mountains Road. (Part of Ivanpah Road and New York Mountains Road are dirt; they are suitable for passenger cars with good ground clearance.) Turn left, west, on New York Mountains Road. A couple OX Cattle Ranch buildings stand near this road's intersection with Ivanpah Road. Drive 5 1/2 miles to an unsigned junction with a dirt road and turn north. Proceed 2 miles to a woodland laced with turnouts that serve as unofficial campsites. Leave your car here; farther along the road dips into a wash and gets very rough.

The walk: From the Caruthers Canyon "Campground" follow the main dirt road up the canyon. As you ascend, look behind you for a great view of Table Mountain, the most dominant peak of the central East Mojave.

Handsome boulders line the trail and frame views of the tall peak before you, New York Mountain. The range's 7,532-foot signature peak is crowned with a botanical island of its own—a relict stand of Rocky Mountain white fir.

A half-mile along, you'll come to a fork in the road. The rightward road climbs a quarter mile to an old mining shack. Take the left fork, dipping in and out of a wash and gaining a great view of the canyon and its castellated walls.

If it's rained recently, you might find water collected in pools on the rocky canyon bottom. Enjoy the tranquility of the gold mine area, but don't stray into the dark, dangerous shafts.

Piute Canyon Trail

5 miles round trip; 600-foot elevation gain

In 1865, Fort Piute was described by a visitor as "a Godforsaken place—the meanest I ever saw for a military station." It's doubtful that many who visit this tiny, lonely Army post today would disagree; however, the ruins of the fort, along with pretty Piute Valley and Piute Creek add up to an intriguing, way off-the-beaten-path tour for the adventurous.

Fort Piute, located east of Lanfair Valley, at the southern end of the Piute Mountains, was established to provide a military presence in the desert, and to protect pioneer travelers on their westward journeys.

Indians resisted the intrusion of settlers on tribal lands; there were frequent attacks on westbound settlers and mail wagons traveling the route from Prescott, Arizona to Los Angeles.

Subsequent military escorts protected travelers, but conditions at the outpost were intolerable for many soldiers stationed at Fort Piute. Desertion was a regular occurrence, and the outpost was officially staffed by just 18 men of the Company "D" 9th Infantry Division from 1867 to 1868.

Today the small, primitive installation lies in ruins; its thick rock and mortar walls have been weathered and crumbled to a height of just two or three feet. The stone outlines of the original buildings delineate three connecting rooms that served as a tiny living quarters, corral and cookhouse.

The walk along Piute Creek is of more than military interest. The only perennial stream in the East Mojave, Piute Creek is an oasis-like area where cottonwoods, willows and sedges flourish. Bighorn sheep frequently visit this watering site, as do a large number of birds. (This is a fragile ecosystem; not a recreation area. Please treat the creek gently.)

The hike explores Piute Creek and gorge and gives you a chance to walk a portion of the historic Mojave Road. Following the Mojave Road Trail, as its called, lets you walk back into time and get a glimpse of the hardships faced by early pioneers.

This is not a hike for the inexperienced or for first-time visitors to the area; the roads and paths are unsigned and sometimes hard to follow.

Experienced hikers and repeat visitors, however, will thoroughly enjoy their exploration of Fort Piute.

Directions to trailhead: Head west on Interstate 40 and take the turnoff for the road leading to the hamlet of Goffs. Pass through Goffs and drive some 16 miles along Lanfair Road to a point about 100 feet beyond its junction with Cedar Canyon Road. Turn right (east) on a road that goes by four names: Cedar Canyon Road, the utility road, Cable Road, Pole Road. The latter three names arise from the fact that the road follows a buried telephone cable. Drive east, staying right at a junction 3.7 miles out, and sticking with the cable road about 6 more miles to another junction where there's a cattle guard. Turn left before the cattleguard on another dirt road and proceed a mile to a corral and the unsigned trailhead.

The walk: From the corral, head almost due south toward a gate, almost a half-mile from the start, which lets you through a fence and onto the old Mojave Road. (Remember to close the gate.)

Now you begin climbing Piute Hill. From atop the hill, catch your breath and admire the view of Table Mountain directly to the west, and Castle Peaks to the north.

One look at the road gives you some idea of the hardships experienced by pioneers who passed this way 130 years ago. Piute Hill, was said to be among the most feared obstacles of the Westward crossing. In 1867, Brigadier General James F. Rusling described the ordeal of crossing the hills as "the worst climb I encountered in my entire tour across the continent."

Hikers can still see the deep ruts carved in the rock by the heavy wagons.

On the way to the fort, you'll pass along loose, sandy trail near Piute Creek, where there's nice picnicking. (The water in the creek is not safe to drink.)

About 1/2 mile from the fort, you'll cross the creek. The Mojave Road narrows. Look sharply for the Piute Canyon Trail coming in from the west. (This will be your optional return route.) Continue on a slight descent to the fort.

An interpretive marker provides some historic information about the history of "Fort Pah Ute, 1867-68." Don't sit on the walls or disturb the ruins; like all cultural resources in the desert, the fort is protected by federal law.

Head back along the Mojave Road one-half mile, bearing right on unsigned Piute Canyon Trail. This narrow path stays high on the canyon wall, heading west at first, then north. A half-mile along, you can see prominent Piute Gorge to the west; you'll be following this gorge back to the trailhead.

The trail is very faint; if you lose the path, keep heading west and descending to the floor of Piute Gorge. Expect a steep scramble to reach the bottom of the gorge.

At the bottom, you'll proceed west up Piute Gorge; stay on the gorge bottom. After a half-mile you'll come to an intersection where another canyon comes in from the left. Don't take this route, but continue up the gorge to the right.

Taking a break amidst the abundant desert flora along the trail to Hole-in-the-Wall.

A little farther, a trail leading out of the gorge takes off from the left. (Keep a sharp eye out for this one.) Take this trail up to the rim of the gorge, where there's a scenic overlook. From here, follow the dirt road south back to the trailhead.

Mid Hills to
Hole-in-the-Wall Trail

***Mid Hills Campground to Hole-in-the-Wall
    Campground***
8 miles one-way with 1,000-foot elevation loss

Hole-in-the-Wall and Mid Hills are the centerpieces of the East Mojave Desert. Both locales offer diverse desert scenery and fine campgrounds.

Doubling the pleasure of these special places is a new, eight mile long trail that links them together. One of the BLM's first major trail projects, the path was constructed by a crew of young men and women of the California Conservation Corps. The Sierra Club has volunteered to maintain the trail.

Mile-high Mid Hills recalls the Great Basin Desert topography of Nevada and Utah. It's a thousand or so feet higher than Hole-in-the-Wall and thus as a starting point offers the hiker an easier way to go.

Mid Hills, so named because of its location halfway between the Providence and New York Mountains, offers a grand observation point from which to gaze out at the East Mojave's dominant mountain ranges: the coffee-with-cream-colored Pinto Mountains to the north, and the rolling Kelso Dunes shining on the western horizon. Looking northwest, you'll also get a superb view of Cima Dome, the 75-square mile chunk of uplifted volcanic rock.

Hole-in-the-Wall is a second inviting locale, the kind of place Butch Cassidy and the Sundance Kid would choose as a hideout.

Hole-in-the-Wall is a twisted maze of red rock. Geologists call this rhyolite, a kind of lava that existed as hot liquid far below the earth's surface, then crystalized.

A series of iron rings aids descent into Banshee Canyon. They're not particularly difficult for those who are reasonably agile and take their time.

If you're not up for a long day hike, the 3/4-mile trip from Hole-in-the-Wall Campground to Banshee Canyon and the 5-mile jaunt to Wildhorse Canyon offer some easier alternatives.

A word about desert hiking in general and this desert hike in particular: You'll often travel in the bottom of sandy washes instead of over more clearly defined trails found in forest locales. This means the hiker must rely on maps, a sense of direction, rock cairns and the very occasional sign.

The hike is an adventurous excursion through a diverse desert environment. You'll see basin and range table-top mesas, large pinyon trees, and colorful cactus and lichen-covered granite rocks. East Mojave views—Table Mountain, Wild Horse Mesa, the Providence Range—are unparalleled.

Directions to trailhead: From Interstate 40, approximately 42 miles west of Needles and nearly 100 miles east of Barstow, exit on Essex Road. Head north 9 1/2 miles to the junction of Essex Road and Black Canyon Road. Bear right on the latter road. After 8 1/2 miles of travel you'll spot Hole-in-the-Wall Campground on your left. Turn

Get a horse! Another way to go from Mid Hills to Hole-in-the-Wall.

When viewed from the trail, Mid Hills seems in the middle of nowhere.

into the campground and park at the lip of Banshee Canyon on the upper loop of the camp road. The unsigned trail plunges right into the canyon.

Those wishing to park vehicles for day hikes on the trail are encouraged to use the Wild Horse Canyon Trailhead on Wild Horse Canyon Road.

Another nine or so miles of travel on Black Canyon Road brings you to the signed turnoff for Mid Hills Campground. Turn left and travel two miles to the campground. The Mid Hills trailhead is located adjacent to a windmill immediately opposite the entrance road to the campground.

The walk: In a short distance, the path ascends to a saddle which offers splendid views of the Pinto Valley to the northeast. (The saddle is this hike's high point.)

From the saddle, the path angles south, descending into, then climbing out of a wash. (Keep a close eye on the trail; it's easy to lose here.)The trail reaches a dirt road, follows it for a mere 100 feet, then turns sharply left to join a wash for a time, exits it, and crosses a road. You encounter another wash, enter it and exit it.

After a modest ascent, the trail joins a road, passes through a gate, and joins another road for a little more than a mile. This road serves up spectacular views to the south of the Providence Mountains and Wild Horse Mesa.

Adjacent to a group of large boulders, a road veers left but hikers bear right, soon turning sharp left with the road. The route passes through another gate, then works its way through a dense thicket of cholla cactus.

After following another wash, the trail crosses a dirt road, then soon joins a second road, which follows a wash to a dead end at an abandoned dam. The trail ascends through some rocks, levels for a time, then descends. A quarter mile before trail's end, you'll spy the Hole-in-the-Wall spur trail leading off to the left.

Step off the trail for close-up views of Nature's handiwork.

Kelso Dunes Trail

Parking area to top of dunes
3 miles roundtrip; 400-foot gain

In the heart of the heart of the East Mojave lie the Kelso Dunes, one of the tallest dune systems in America.

And the dunes give off good vibrations, say many desert day hikers.

The good vibrations that enthuse hikers are not the desert's spiritual emanations—which many visitors find considerable—but the Kelso Dunes' rare ability to make a low rumbling sound when sand slides down the steep slopes. This sound has been variously described as that of a kettle drum, low flying airplane or Tibetan gong.

The sand that forms Kelso Dunes blows in from the Mojave River basin. After traveling east 35 miles across a stark plane known as the Devil's Playground, it's deposited in hills nearly 600 feet high. The westerlies carrying the sand rush headlong into winds from other directions, which is why the sand is dropped here, and stays here.

For further confirmation of the circular pattern of winds that formed the dunes, examine the bunches of grass on the lower slopes. You'll notice that the tips of the tall grasses have etched 360-degree circles on the sand.

Other patterns on the sand are made by the desert's abundant, but rarely seen, wildlife. You might see the tracks of a coyote, kit fox, antelope ground squirrel, packrat, raven or sidewinder. Footprints of lizards and mice can be seen tacking this way and that over the sand. The dune's surface records the lightest pressure of the smallest feet.

Directions to trailhead: From Interstate 15 in Baker, some 60 miles northeast of Barstow, turn south on Kelbaker Road and proceed about 35 miles to the town of Kelso. Pause to admire the classic neo-Spanish style Kelso Railroad Depot next to the Union Pacific tracks.

From Kelso, continue on Kelbaker Road for another 7 miles to a signed dirt road and turn west (right). Drive slowly along this road (navigable for all but very low slung passenger cars) 3 miles to a parking area. The trail to Kelso Dunes begins just up the dirt road from the parking area.

The walk: Only the first quarter-mile or so of the walk to the dunes is on established trail. Once the trail peters out, angle toward the low saddle atop the dunes, just to the right of the highest point.

Know the old saying "One step forward, two steps back"? This saying will take on new meaning if you attempt to take the most direct route to the top of the dunes by walking straight up the tallest sand hill.

As you cross the lower dunes, you'll pass some mesquite and creosote bushes. During spring of a good wildflower year, the lower dunes are bedecked with yellow and white desert primrose, pink sand verbena and yellow sunflowers.

When you reach the saddle located to the right of the high point, turn left and trek another hundred yards or so to the top. The black material crowning the top of the dunes is magnetite, an iron oxide, and one of about two dozen minerals found within the dune system.

Enjoy the view from the top: the Kelso Mountains to the north, the Bristol Mountains to the southwest, the Granite Mountains to the south, the Providence Mountains to the east. Everywhere you look there are mountain ranges, small and large.

In fact, despite evidence to the contrary—most notably the stunning dunes beneath your feet—the East Mojave is really a desert of mountains not sand.

While atop the dunes, perhaps your footsteps will cause mini-avalanches and the dunes will sha-boom-sha-boom for you. There's speculation that the extreme dryness of the East Mojave, combined with the wind-polished, rounded nature of the individual sand grains, has something to do with their musical ability. After picking up good

Shaboom-shaboom! Good times on the booming Kelso dunes.

vibrations, descend the steep dune face (much easier on the way down!) and return to the trailhead.

Mitchell Caverns Trail

1 1/2 miles round trip

Trail trivia question: Where in Southern California can you explore some stunning scenery, be assured that it won't rain, and know that the temperature for your hike will always be a comfortable 65 degrees?

Hint: One of the overlooked gems of the California state park system, an island of state-owned land in the vast federal dominion.

If you're in the dark, then you're on the right path—the trail through Mitchell Caverns State Reserve, part of Providence Mountains State Recreation Area. Ranger-led walks through the dramatic limestone caves offer a fascinating geology lesson, one the whole family can enjoy.

In 1932, Jack Mitchell abandoned his Depression-shattered business in Los Angeles and moved to the desert. For a time he prospected for silver, but his real fascination was with what he called the "Providence" or "Crystal Caves" and their potential as a tourist attraction. He constructed several stone buildings to use for lodging. (Today's park visitors center is one of these buildings.) Mitchell and his wife Ida provided food, lodging, and guided tours of the caverns until 1954. By all accounts, Jack Mitchell was quite a yarn spinner. Older Southern Californians still remember his tall tales of ghosts, lost treasure and bottomless pits.

Now that the caverns are part of the state park system, rangers lead the tours. They're an enthusiastic lot and quite informative. Visitors walk through the two main caves, which Mitchell named El Pakiva (The Devil's House) and Tecopa (after a Chemehuevi chieftain). You'll get a close-up view of stalactites and stalagmites, cave ribbon, cave spaghetti and flow stone. And you'll learn about some of the caverns' former inhabitants—

the Chemhuevi Indians and a Pleistocene ground sloth who stumbled into the darkness some 15,000 years ago.

During Jack Mitchell's day, visitors had to be nimble rock climbers and wait for their tour leader to toss flares into the darkness. Nowadays, the caverns are equipped with stairs and special lighting.

Guided (fee) tours are conducted Monday through Friday at 1:30 p.m. On Saturday and Sunday, tours begin at 10:00 a.m., 1:30 p.m. and 3:00 p.m. A tour takes 1 1/2 to 2 hours depending on your group's enthusiasm and collective curiosity.

Directions to trailhead: From Interstate Highway 40, about eighty miles east of Barstow, exit on Essex Road and drive 16 miles to road's end to the Providence Mountains State Recreation Area. Sign up at the Visitors Center for tours.

Other trails: Because you can only tour the caverns with a park ranger and because you wouldn't want us to spoil the many surprises of the cave walk with a step by step description, we won't further detail the Mitchell Caverns Trail. However, after exploring "the great indoors" allow some time to explore the park's outdoors pathways.

Pick up an interpretive booklet from the park visitors center and walk the half-mile long Mary Beal Nature Trail, which offers a great introduction to high desert flora. Cliff rose and blue sage share the hillsides with cholla, catsclaw and creosote.

The trail honors Mary Beal, a Riverside librarian who at the turn of the century was "exiled" to the desert by her doctor for health reasons. For a half-century this remarkable woman wandered through the Providence Mountains and other remote Mojave Desert locales in order to gather and classify hundreds of varieties of plants and wildflowers.

The short Overlook Trail leads from the park's tiny campground to a viewpoint, which offers vistas of Clipper Valley, the Marble Mountains, and hundreds of square miles of basin and range.

The one-mile long Crystal Springs Trail travels into the pinyon pine- and juniper-dotted Providence Mountains by way of Crystal Canyon. Bighorn sheep are often spotted in this canyon.

CHAPTER TWENTY-ONE

Resources

Desert Information Center
831 Barstow Road
Barstow, CA 92311
(619) 256-8313

Calico Early Man Archeological
   Site
P.O. 535
Yermo, CA 92398

Citizens for Mojave National
   Park
P.O. Box 106
Barstow, CA 92311

Desert Protective Council
   Foundation
P.O. Box 76210
Los Angeles, CA 90076

Desert Studies Center
Course Information:
c/o Office of Extended
   Education
CSU San Bernardino
San Bernardino, CA 92407
(714) 887-7667
or
Biology Department
CSU Fullerton
Fullerton, CA 92634
(714) 773-2428

Desert Tortoise Council
5319 Cerritos Avenue
Long Beach, CA 90805

Friends of the Mojave Road
P.O. Box 307
Norco, CA 91760

Kelso Depot Fund
P.O. Box 35
Kelso, CA 92351

Mojave River Valley Museum
270 East Virginia Way
Barstow, CA 92311

Nipton Station
Route #1
P.O. Box 357
Nipton, CA 92364
(619) 856-2335

Providence Mountains State
   Recreation Area
Post Office Box 1
Essex, Ca 92332-0001

U.S. Bureau of Land Management

California Desert District
6221 Box Spring Blvd.
Riverside, CA 92507
(909) 697-5200

Needles Resource Area
101 W. Spike's Road
Needles, CA 92363
(619) 326-3896

Camping Information

Afton Canyon Campground
38 miles east of Barstow via I-15,
   3 miles south on Afton Canyon
   Road
22 sites

Barstow/Calico KOA
   Campground
exit I-15 at Ghost Town Road
P.O. Box 967
Yermo, CA 92398
(619) 254-2311
72 sites

Calico/San Bernardino County
   Regional Park
exit I-15 at Ghost Town Road
3 miles north
(619) 254-2122
250 sites, no hook-ups

Hole-in-the-Wall Campground
16 miles northwest of Essex via
   Essex Road, 19 miles north on
   Black Canyon Road
20 sites

Mid-Hills Campground
16 miles northwest of Essex via
   Essex Road, 19 miles north on
   Black Canyon Road
20 sites

Needles KOA
exit I-40 at W. Broadway.River
   Road, then 1/34 miles north via
   River Road and Old National
   Trails Highway
P.O. Box 175
Needles, CA 92363
(619) 326-4207
88 sites

Owl Canyon BLM Campground
8 miles north of Barstow via Camp
   Irwin Road, 2 miles west on
   Fossil Beds Road
31 sites

You can't camp at the Needles train staion, even today, but there are plenty of places in the East Mojave to pitch your tent and park your rig.

Desert Reading

An eclectic assortment of classic and contemporary work, including natural history notes, novels and thought-provoking essays

Desert Solitaire: A Season in the Wilderness
Edward Abbey
McGraw-Hill Book Company, 1968

Blue Desert
Charles Bowden
University of Arizona Press, 1986

The Joshua Tree
Robert Cabot
North Atlantic Books, 1970

California Desert Trails
Joseph Smeaton Chase
Originally published by Houghton Mifflin, 1919
reprinted by Tioga Publishing Company, 1987

The Thousand-Mile Summer
Colin Fletcher
Random House, 1964

The California Deserts
Edmund C. Jaeger
Stanford University Press, 1933
Desert Passages: Encounters with the American Deserts
Patricia Nelson Limerick
University of New Mexico, 1985

Desert Notes: Reflections in the Eye of a Raven
Barry Holstun Lopez
Avon Books, 1976

Basin and Range
John McPhee
Farrar Straus Giroux, 1980

Gathering the Desert
Gary Paul Nabhan
The University of Arizona Press, 1987

Unassigned Territory
Kem Nunn
Dell Publishing Company, 1987

Southwest Classics: The Creative Literature of the Arid Lands
Lawrence Clark Powell
Capra Press, 1974

The Desert
John C. Van Dyke
Peregrine Smith, Inc., 1980

INDEX

Other books in the *Walking the West* series:

Walking Los Angeles
Walking Santa Barbara
Walking Southern California
Walking the California Coast
Walking California's State Parks